SACRED COWS

Make Gourmet Burgers

Sacred Cows Make Gourmet Burgers

Ministry Anytime,
Anywhere,
by Anybody

WILLIAM M. EASUM

ABINGDON PRESS / Nashville

SACRED COWS MAKE GOURMET BURGERS
Ministry Anytime, Anywhere, by Anybody

This book is printed on recycled, acid-free paper.

Library of Congress Cataloging-in-Publication Data

Easum, William M., 1939–
  Sacred cows make gourmet burgers : ministry anytime, anywhere, by anybody / William Easum.
     p.   cm.
  ISBN 0-687-00563-9 (pbk. : alk. paper)
  1. Christian leadership. 2. Control (Psychology_—Religious aspects—Christianity—Controversial literature. 3. Pastoral theology. I. Title.
  BV652.1.E18   1995
253—dc20   95-22446
                                                                      CIP

Scripture quotations are taken from the New Revised Standard Version Bible, Copyright 1989 by the Division of Christian Education of the National Council of the Churches of Christ in the USA. Used by Permission.

01 02 03 04 — 10 9

MANUFACTURED IN THE UNITED STATES OF AMERICA

WHAT'S INSIDE

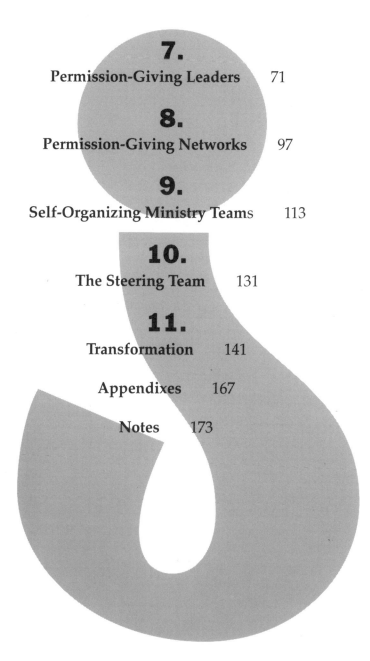

A Personal Comment

In 1986, Dr. Kennon Callahan was serving as our consultant at Colonial Hills Church, helping us to develop our long-range plan. He and I were sitting in my study discussing my future. I shared with him that it was my lifelong dream to write a book, but I couldn't get my story on paper. "Why don't you do a couple of seminars and the book will probably fall into place," he counseled. Six months later, I did my first seminar, and a year later *The Church Growth Handbook* was finished. I will always be indebted to Dr. Callahan for his help in the early years of my development as a consultant.

Since that evening with Dr. Callahan, three additional books have developed from my seminars. Each book builds on the previous book, yet each stands alone.

The Church Growth Handbook is an attempt to help plateaued or declining, program-based, established churches find the will to reach out to the unchurched around them. The book is clearly designed for fragile, established Christians focused on themselves. It is a basic book, comparable to learning the alphabet.

My second book, *How to Reach Baby Boomers*, was born out of an earlier struggle in the seventies to understand why things that worked in the early years of my ministry no longer worked. This book explains the differences between people born before and after 1946 and the ministries that reach people born after 1946. It scratches the surface of the major changes in effective ministry. It also brings to the surface the resistance and conflict that often accompany change in fragile, established churches. This book is comparable to learning how to make sentences out of the alphabet.

Dancing with Dinosaurs, my third book, goes far beyond the traditional established church and describes the

"Fringe Christians" and paradigms pointing the way to the future. It openly acknowledges the demise of fragile, traditional, established congregations and begins describing the church of the twenty-first century. This book is comparable to writing paragraphs out of sentences.

Sacred Cows Make Gourmet Burgers is a response to the many questions and comments about control made by church leaders in my consultations with local churches and in my seminars. Most of the questions seem to be based on the assumption that everything that happens in the church has to be controlled and coordinated.

All four books radiate out from a central theme: life in Christ comes to us on its way to someone else, congregations should focus outward instead of inward, congregations exist for those who are not part of them, life is meant to be given away not kept, God does not honor congregations that seek merely to raise money and survive.

To write *Sacred Cows Make Gourmet Burgers* I had to jump into two worlds I knew little about—physiology and quantum physics. The journey was fascinating and rewarding. A special thanks goes to two people: Dr. David Green, a physician and friend, who introduced me to the intricacies of the human body; and Dr. Tony Amos, an Islander and oceanographer who pointed me to the books I needed to read about quantum theory. This book is comparable to writing an essay out of paragraphs.

I hope that as you read you begin to smell hamburger cooking somewhere in your own ministry. Perhaps the following pages may convince your church leaders that it is better to free the people of God to make responsible contributions to the Body of Christ than to continue to control what happens in the congregation. If it even begins the conversion, it was worth the effort.

Yours in Christ,
Bill Easum
Port Aransas, Texas

CHAPTER 1

THE SACRED COW

"It is easier to ask for forgiveness than it is to get permission."
B. R. Hagebak

Established churches worship at the feet of the sacred cow of CONTROL. Control takes many shapes; our insistence on controlling everything that happens in our congregations and denominations; our desire to coordinate everything that happens, or to know about everything before it happens, or to insist on voting on every new issue or ministry; a parlor that few people use; a gym floor that must be kept scratch free; a kitchen that no one can use but designated persons; money that belongs to the Trustees; an official body that has to approve every de-cision. Control is stifling the spiritual growth of God's people.

In the local church, control is exercised by a handful of laity. Within denominations, control is exercised by the clergy. The laity stifle growth within the local church, and the clergy do so within the denomination.[1]

Established churches must either cease worshiping the god of control, or they perish!

> *This book is about freeing individuals and teams to make responsible contributions to the Body of Christ without having to first ask for permission*

The Body of Christ is most effective when individuals are given permission to live out their God-given spiritual gifts (described in chapter 6) on behalf of the Body rather than someone restraining what they can or cannot do. This book is about freeing individuals and teams to make responsible contributions to the Body of Christ without having to first ask for permission.[2]

The freedom of individuals to act responsibly and make a contribution to the Body of Christ does not happen through representative democracy as most established churches seem to believe. Electing people to vote on behalf of those who elected them encourages responsible action only in a very select few. People can't act responsibly and make a contribution unless they are free to control things that are important to them.[3] People are free to be responsible only when they do not have to go through a labyrinth of committees to get approval. Representative government does little to involve ordinary people in designing the organization, planning its strategy and tactics, or making decisions about things that vitally effect their lives. If people want to start new ministries in which they live out their spiritual gifts, they should be free to do so.

However, in worship of the sacred cow of control church leaders cry:

"We've never done it that way before."
"We tried that before and it didn't work."
"No one does THAT in this church."
"We don't do things that way."
"It's too radical a change for us."
"If only it were that easy."
"When you've been around longer, you'll understand why it can't be done."
"How dare you criticize what we're doing."
"We've been running this church since long before you were born."
"Who gave you permission to change the rules?"
"What you're suggesting is against our policies."
"Our church law won't let us do that."
"Won't that open us up to liability?"

Webster defines a sacred cow as "one immune from criticism or attack." The term comes from the Hindu veneration of the cow. Sacred cows are more important than people, causing some people to literally starve to death while surrounded by their sacred cows. No one ever considers the possibility of using the cows for food. To suggest doing so is sacrilegious.

> **Making decisions and controlling what happens is more important in estalished churches than making disciples.**

Thousands of persons have attended my seminars. During the presentations, I see many eyes light up with excitement as we explore new possibilities for ministry. Then reality sets in. The participants begin to ask, "How will we get these new ideas past those who control the decision-making process in our church? They know instinctively that the leadership will say "No" to the new ministry. The participants become so fixated on the issue of control that their excitement about the potential of the new ministry is dampened.

I once thought that church leaders were exaggerating how difficult it was going to be when they returned home and tried to implement new ministries. Now, I'm convinced that making decisions and controlling what happens is more important in established churches than making disciples. Two real life examples explain why even the Great Commission is thwarted by institutional gridlock.

In Church A, the worship attendance in the single service has been going up and down in yo-yo fashion for the past ten years. The top end of the yo-yo is between 80 and 85 percent capacity of their worship space. During this time, the membership began to approach an average age of sixty, while the average age in the community is thirty-five.

The solution is simple. Church A needs to add a second worship service designed to reach unchurched people between thirty and forty years of age. The church leaders gave the recommendation to the existing Worship Committee. One of the committee members is the Music Director, who is well-trained in classical music. After six months of unhappy meetings, the Worship Committee decides to recommend the second service. However, when they take the request to their official body, they are told they must first talk with the Finance and Trustee Committees. Both committees have just met the previous week, so the Worship Committee has to wait another month. It turns out that the two committees decide to meet on the same night, making it impossible for the Worship Committee to meet with both. The Worship Committee meets with the Finance Committee who gives them approval. When the Worship

Committee meets with the Trustees a month later, they discover that the Trustees want them to receive bids on the needed sound equipment before deciding on the issue.

> *Control is the Sacred Cow of established churches, and it needs to be ground into gourmet hamburger.*

The Worship Committee is now into the ninth month since the recommendation was made. The ninth month happens to be July, and the worship attendance drops as it always does. The tenth month the Worship Committee meets with the Trustees to find that they do not see the need for this service since attendance is so low. So, the Trustees ask the Worship Committee to monitor the worship attendance and talk with them again in two months.

In the twelfth month the Worship Committee meets again with the Trustees only to discover that the Music Director has met with them the month before and pleaded her case for not designing the service for unchurched people between thirty and forty. She does not consider the "shallow and frivolous" music appropriate to services in the church. The Trustees tell the Worship Committee they cannot approve the issue until the official body votes on for whom the service is to be designed and what kind of music would be used.

By now several people on the Worship Committee are upset with each other and with the Music Director. In desperation the Worship Committee chair resigns. A new person cannot be appointed until the coming year, so the new worship service dies for lack of energy.

A second example involves the nursery. Church B is over one hundred years old and has been declining in membership for thirty years. However, it is still a church with over 400 in worship. The past three years young couples began buying up homes in the area and remodeling them. Two or three of these young couples have joined the church and asked the church to provide a better nursery.

At the height of Church B's history, the nursery was across the hall from the worship center. However, thirty years ago it had been moved to the basement, and for the past ten years has been closed. Presently, it is used as a storage room. The basement is also damp and musty.

The young couples approach the pastor about starting a nursery, returning it to its original place, and providing a paid sitter. The pastor tells them they have to talk with the Trustee Committee because what they want involves the use of the facilities, and they have to talk with the Finance Committee because the move involves money. The couples take a deep breath.

The Trustees say that the nursery could be started, but it had to remain in the basement because the women's organization maintains the old nursery location as a parlor. "The parlor isn't used much," they say, "but the women have put a lot of money into making it a lovely place." The Finance Committee would not authorize any funds for a paid sitter, because the members did not need a paid sitter when they were young.

The nursery is reestablished in the basement. However, a few things still must be stored in it; the basement is still damp; the carpet still has stains of unmentionable origin. The young couples offer to spend their own money to decorate the nursery and pay a sitter, but the board replies that the church does not encourage designated giving.

Two years and several thousand new couples in the area later, the church continues to decline and grow older, and the few young couples that had once been members moved on to a more friendly environment. A report came to me from the defeated pastor that the church leadership was convinced that they had done the right thing by refusing to spend the money to move the nursery and pay a sitter. After all, the young couples weren't committed enough in the first place or they wouldn't have left!

Control is the Sacred Cow of established churches, and it needs to be ground into gourmet hamburger.

If you are working harder at ministry and getting farther behind, and it pains you, this book will relieve your pain. If you are a church leader who yearns for the days when your church was vibrant and alive, this book is for you. If you are an unchurched person looking for significant meaning for your life, this book will describe the kind of church you need to find. If you are comfortable with the way things are in your church, this book will probably cause discomfort. However, discomfort is often the prelude to resurrection.

How to Use This Book

This book is designed to help you lay a foundation for ministry for the rest of your life. It is a book about how to develop effective ministries in an emerging new world. It is a book about new skills. It is not a "how to" book.

Some readers may wish that more specific examples of ministry were included. This would violate the spirit

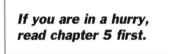

If you are in a hurry, read chapter 5 first.

of the emerging new world. Instead of offering prepackaged programs or quick fixes, I offer you the context in which to discover your own ministries and long-term solutions.

If you are in a hurry, or do not care about theological and cultural foundations, go directly to chapter 5. Then read chapters 7 through 9. Then return to chapters 1 through 4. If you are then ready to act on what you have read, read chapters 10 and 11. Also, to help speed the reading process, I have used many contractions.

Many of the endnotes contain more than just references to quotations. I have placed important, explanatory material in the endnotes instead of the body of the text to enhance the flow of thought.

Every now and then a **moo** will appear. It is my hope that every time you see it you will smell hamburgers cooking somewhere.

You will benefit the most by reading the book the first time in a safe environment with a friend. This prepares you to experience the team approach to ministry described in chapter 9. Set aside time to get together at intervals to compare notes and explore the interaction of your thoughts. Challenge each other to reflect more deeply on the implications of what you've just read. This helps you establish the learning loop described in chapter 11. If you see new insights into how to do away with the sacred cow of control, write me. This develops the network described throughout the book.[4]

When you see a reference to Colonial Hills Church, I am referring to the church I lead between 1969 and 1993. It was a nine-year-old church with 37 in worship and the people in the midst of bankruptcy when I arrived. By 1993, it had reached an average attendance of just under 1,000 in worship.

A New Form of Church

A new form of congregational life is dragging Christians kicking and screaming into the twenty-first century. The self-understanding, focus, corporate culture, leadership, organizational styles, and strategies are radically different from those experienced throughout the twentieth century. The future church offers new opportunities and problems and requires a new mindset.

This new form of congregational life is with us now. I call it the *permission-giving network*.

CHAPTER 2

THE QUANTUM AGE

"No one born in 1990 could possibly imagine the world in which one's grandparents had grown up, or the world in which one's own parents had been born."

Peter Drucker

We live in a time unlike any other time that any living person has known. It's not merely that things are changing. Change itself has changed, thereby changing the rules by which we live.[1]

Established Protestantism was born into the Industrial Age, a world of slow, incremental change. Enormous changes, such as the combustible engine, did occur, but they came far enough apart that no matter how slowly church leaders responded, ample time remained to assimilate the implications. The devastating results of our slow response to these changes went unnoticed because of the gradual evolution of change.

The Industrial Age was a machine-driven world in which the primary machine was the combustible engine. Newtonian or classical physics was at the heart of this world. It examined reality as if it were a machine. Classical physics focused on "things" and how to break them down into separate parts. By breaking "things" down into their parts and dissecting them, the whole could be understood. A combustible engine was nothing more than the

> **Change itself has changed.**

19

IMAGES OF THE INDUSTRIAL WORLD

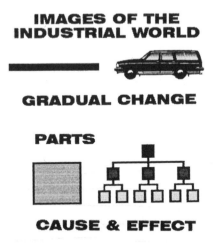

GRADUAL CHANGE

PARTS

CAUSE & EFFECT

sum of all its parts. Understand the parts and how they fit together, and you understand the engine.

Once programmed, this giant, predictable machine functioned according to the rules of the program. Every cause had an effect. This world was based on balance, equilibrium, and linear motion and thinking. Since reality consisted of "things," and was understood by dissecting the parts, space was considered empty and lonely. In this type of existence, bureaucracies, spans of control, and entitlement worked well.

Somewhere in the middle of the twentieth century, all of this changed. Change occurred, not in incremental steps, but in random, episodic, discontinuous, quantum leaps. According to Zbigniew Brezezinski, "we live in a world that is already in fact very different from the one which we have begun to comprehend, and by the time our comprehension has caught up with the new reality, the world is likely to be even more drastically different in ways that today may seem unthinkable."[2]

> Our slow response to the changing needs of the human spirit is taking an enormous toll.

The result of this discontinuous change has been disastrous for established church leaders. Ministries and styles of leadership that once appeared to work well no longer produce the desired results. Church leaders work harder and get farther behind. Across the board, denominational organization is in a downward spiral. Our slow response to the changing needs of the human spirit is taking an enormous toll.

Peter Drucker warned us in 1969 that we were entering a world of discontinuity in which the world of slow, incremental change would be replaced by a world of fast, revolutionary change.[3] In 1981, Alvin Toffler extended Drucker's caution by exposing the patterns of a world that was not developing continuously but was entering a totally new stage of development, a new wave.[4] Harrison Owen talked about the "world of raplexity" in which rapid and complex change takes the place of slow, incremental change.[5]

> **Nothing in our past prepared us for the present.**

However, there is more to this change than simply a linear extrapolation of rapid change and complexity. Quantum leaps are happening that are nothing like evolution. They remove us almost totally from our previous context. Simply learning to do old chores faster or to be able to adapt old forms to more complex situations no longer produces the desired results.

Improving our communication doesn't help either. Computers have taught us that whenever we increase the speed and complexity of one part of a system, all other parts of the system will slow down relative to the increased speed and complexity of the others. Running harder and harder in ministry will not work in this new world.

In 1988, Igor Ansoff argued that we needed an organization that could cope not so much with extraordinary changes as with a different kind of change. He said: "A change is discontinuous if it does not directly follow the historical logic of the firm's development."

Established churches are becoming increasingly ineffective because our past has not prepared us for ministry in the future. The discontinuity we have experienced because of these quantum leaps is comparable to the experience of the residents of East Berlin when the Berlin Wall came down. Nothing in their past prepared them for life without the Wall. Very little in our past has prepared us for ministry in today's world.

The Quantum Age

A new economy and world view are emerging, which are driven by two new disciplines—quantum physics and microprocessors. Both disciplines approach knowledge and reality in a radically different way from classical physics. Quantum physics seeks to understand the system as well as the relationships that exist between the parts. The whole is understood to be more than the sum of the parts because of the *relationships* between the parts.[6]

The qualitative measurements that were so crucial to the Newtonian world are giving way to qualitative sensitivities of a new world. That objects exist is less important than that they are in relationship. What a person *is*, is less important than what a person *is becoming*. The deductive reasoning of the Newtonian world cannot prove the existence of God, but the inductive reasoning of quantum physics can notice a consistent, unexplainable "benevolence" to the course of human experience.[7]

The relationships between the parts consist of invis-

22

ible fields that fill all of space and are observable to us only through their effects. Cyberspace, the term used to describe an atmosphere filled with electronic information, is one of these fields. The correlation of electrons is another. Space is alive with relationships, each one affecting the other no matter how far removed.[8] "Nothing happens in quantum physics without something encountering something else."[9] These relationships determine what one observes and how particles manifest themselves.[10]

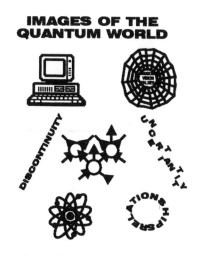

IMAGES OF THE QUANTUM WORLD

Who I am is tied to what you are, and, in the final analysis, to the nature of the tree in my backyard and the volcano erupting on the Pacific Rim. All reality participates in the constitution of all other reality. If you change the course of an atom in one quadrant of the universe, it changes the course of another atom in another quadrant of the universe.

While in the Newtonian world inertia was the norm of the universe until some object struck another object, in the quantum world change is the norm of the universe. No constants exist. A radical unpredictability underlies all experience and a profound irrationality lies at the heart of experience.

This new world is alive with varying potentials that can never be understood or chronicled until they are measured. Living and changing networks replace non-thinking machines. Linear thinking is replaced with interactive thought. Unlike the Newtonian world, the quantum world does not have predetermined destinations as a result of our actions. Instead of cause and effect, it offers potentials depending on how someone or something comes into relationship with the event. Every situation has many potential results.

This means that objective reality is not as verifiable and predictable as was thought in the Newtonian world. All that exists is what we create by the relationships into which we enter with others and various events. Everything comes into being as it is observed in relationship to someone else or some other thing. Everything is connected. Nothing stands alone. To some physicists, relationships are the "stuff" of reality. Some biologists even see the earth as a living organism, which is actively engaged in creating the conditions that support life.[11]

> **Relationships are the "stuff" of reality.**

Quantum physics presents us with an orderly world of paradoxes where either side of the paradox could be correct, depending on its relationship to another. There is no "either/or," only potentials that materialize based on the interaction of relationships. There is no need to decide between polarities. We need to focus on the relationship between the two. Thus, absolutes and uniformity do not exist. Truth and order are not immutable; they are based on the interaction of individuals. This new world offers a serious challenge to those of us who believe in a never-changing God behind everything that exists.   mOO

When scientists began exploring the world of atomic physics, they found that every time they asked a question, their experiments gave them a paradoxical answer. When they tried to clarify the experiment, the paradox became greater. It wasn't long before they realized that quantum physics required a new approach. As soon as they accepted the existence of paradox as a natural part of atomic physics, they began to ask the right questions. Soon, quantum theory emerged.

> **The effect of Quantum theory on the scientific world has been shattering.**

The effect of quantum theory on the scientific world has been shattering.[12] Many of the discoveries of quantum physics cannot be explained by Newtonian physics, and almost everything scientists once believed is being called into question.

Newton's Second Law of Thermodynamics is one of the long accepted laws of nature called into question by this new science. This law says that sooner or later all systems or forces disintegrate. Quantum physics asserts just the opposite.[13] Things in the environment that disturb a system's equilibrium help create new forms of order. Chaos or disorder become the source of new order instead of something to be avoided. Chaos is desirable because it is the start of something new. Organizations, over time, do not have to wind down and go out of existence if they embrace the chaos and learn a new way to achieve old things. (We will see how this chaos theory affects established Protestantism in chapter 8.)

The Industrial Age focused on the parts, but the Quantum Age focuses on the whole. The Industrial Age was concerned with linear thinking and cause and effect, but the Quantum Age is concerned with the interconnectedness of all of the parts and their relationships. The Industrial Age saw clearly defined compartments of life all neatly functioning, but the Quantum Age realizes that there are no natural boundaries, only those that we create when we walk into a new time or space, because everything in the universe is connected to everything else. In the Industrial Age chaos was to be avoided, but in the Quantum Age chaos leads to a new order. Hierarchy was the backbone of the Industrial Age, but networks are more important in the Quantum Age. In the industrial society paper money was basic, but the Quantum Age uses an intangible medium of exchange known as the electronic funds transfer system. In the Industrial Age service was a category of business among many others, but in the Quantum Age service is an essential ingredient of every business.

The following chart shows the fundamental differences between the Industrial and the Quantum Ages.

NEWTONIAN WORLD	QUANTUM WORLD
Linear thought	Interconnectedness
Boundaries	Varying boundaries
Avoid chaos	Embrace chaos
Hierarchy	Networks
Paper money	Electronic funds
Service sector	Service inherent
Machines	Organic
Automobile	Microprocessors
Parts	Relationships
Evolution	Discontinuity
Cause and effect	Unrealized potentials
Static process	Dynamic process
Objective reality	No objective reality
Things	Organic
Entropy	Dissipation
What is it?	How does it work?

Along with this new world view, a new economy is emerging that is changing the way people view reality and process knowledge. Today, the microprocessor drives the new economy as powerfully as the internal combustion engine drove the Industrial Age. Between 1990 and 1993, more money was spent on computers and communication equipment than on all other capital equipment combined. Just as the internal combustible engine pumped life into the old world, the microprocessor is the vital organ of the Quantum Age.

The development of databases gives us an insight into the tremendous change in the way knowledge is processed in the Quantum Age. Databases were first designed hierarchically. If you wanted to create a database of churches, pastors, denominations, and various ministries, you had to predetermine which of these subjects you wanted to sort first, second, third, and fourth. The printout would look like a hierarchial organization chart. To find one child in one classroom might take several searches through several levels of information.

The discovery of "quantum chips" may lead to the development of artificial intelligence.

Today, information can be read in any order or level without searching through each one separately. Each of the above subjects or levels of information all belong to the whole, and each student belongs to all four levels simultaneously. This parallel processing abandons a linear step-by-step sequencing of information for a simultaneous approach where many processors handle different parts of a job at the same time.

The marriage of computers and quantum mechanics may prove to be the most radical change in the twenty-first century. Because computer chips are be-

> *Instead of being encased in fluid and covered with skin as is the brain, this "not so artificial intelligence" will be encased in a quantum chip covered by artificial, human skin.*

coming smaller and smaller, the time will come when a "quantum chip" the size of an atom is developed. The operation of these chips will occur on such a tiny scale that the laws governing their operations will be based, not on Newtonian physics, but on the principles of quantum physics. This requires a new form of logic which will make possible many new applications of present day knowledge. When this happens, the unseen quantum world will be at the fingertips of the user. This discovery will open many new potential answers to some of our most eternal questions, as is being suggested in Frank J. Tipler's *The Physics of Immortality*.[14]

The discovery of "quantum chips" may lead to the development of a thinking computer. Today's computers are limited to performing difficult and complex calculations, but tomorrow's computers may have powers rivaling those of the human brain. Instead of doing tasks, computers will think through problems. Instead of simply analyzing data and processing information, they will be able to reason through to solutions and create software needed to process new information. Instead of being encased in fluid and covered with skin as is the brain, this "not so artificial intelligence" will be encased in a quantum chip covered by artificial, human skin.

So What?

Church leaders in the Quantum Age must do everything they can to slaughter the sacred cow of control.

Tightly controlled organizations and institutions will not do well in the Quantum Age. The top-down oppressive approach of bureaucracy is on its m00 way out. In its place are emerging *permission-giving networks*. These networks are freeing and empowering people to explore their spiritual gifts individually and in teams on behalf of the Body of Christ.

The quantum world, like the Scriptures, focuses on accountability as opposed to control. Accountability occurs *after* action takes place. The individual or team takes action and then gives an account of what was done and why it was done. Control occurs *before* a person or team takes action. The individual or team has to ask for permission before taking action. In the quantum world, church leaders must develop an environment in which accountability more than control guides the direction of ministry.

However, the struggle to minister effectively in the Quantum Age will not be an easy task because of the Controllers. We learn about them in the next chapter.

CHAPTER 3

THE CONTROLLERS

"This is our church and we'll decide who can use it!"

Chair of Trustees

"That music will never be sung in this church!"

Director of Music

The life and spirit of established churches is being drained by mean-spirited people called *Controllers*. Controllers are those leaders who withhold permission or make it difficult for new ministries to start. Control and the abuse of power and authority have no place in the Body of Christ. It is time for us to either convert or neutralize the Controllers.[1] **moo**

When I first began consulting, I thought that the sacred cow was "maintaining the status quo."[2] The more I work with congregations, the more I realize that keeping the status quo is merely the tip of an iceberg.

I arrived at this conversion after several years of helping congregations start contemporary or alternative worship services. Instead of encouraging churches to gradually change an existing service, I encourage them to begin an alternate service designed for people born after World War Two. Thus, no changes have to be made in the existing service, producing a "win-win"

> *Controllers not only do not want change; they also want to control everything that happens.*

situation. I remind them over and over that no one must go to this new service who does not desire it. They can continue to go to their present service. All they need do is give permission for this new service to begin.

If change or status quo were the sacred cow, this strategy would work with minimum controversy. However, it still causes conflict. Controllers not only do not want change; they also want to control everything that happens. If the new ministry is not what they want and need, they make sure it does not happen. They work so hard at keeping bad things from happening that nothing new ever happens. Paranoia over past mistakes and future errors have led to a highly controlled atmosphere.

Every church I have worked with as a consultant has been filled with good people who care about each other. That is their strength; it is also their weakness. They are so good they will put up with people that no one else on earth will put up with. Because of their goodness, they attract a handful of neurotic, mean-spirited, self-centered people who do everything in their power to control what happens in the church. When the church finally gets fed up with them and does something they do not like, over their heated protest, they get mad and leave the church. Almost every church that begins to grow after a long-term decline experiences someone storming out of the church during the transition. **mOO**

Controllers make sure that new church members serve in areas where "they" want them to serve. If there is an opening in the youth group or a need for a Sunday school teacher, or an opening on a minor committee, Controllers encourage them to fill the vacancy which the church needs filled. Even then the new people do not have authority to make decisions. They must ask permission from another group that is usually made up of older, longtime members.

My experience has taught me that the Trustees, Music Director, worship committee, choir, and nonofficial leaders are the main Controllers in the church.   moo

For example, a church with over 400 in worship had been declining for twenty years. The Official Board spent three hours debating about buying a fax machine. Finally, one of the members offered to pay for the machine as a means to end the argument. Instead of having the Church Administrator install the machine, the Trustees were asked to decide how to install it. Three months and two meetings later the fax machine was installed. How it was installed is worse than how long it took. The church had only two phone lines, which is not enough for a church of that size. The cost of adding a third line dedicated to the fax would cost thirty-five dollars. Instead of adding a third line, the trustees took one of the two lines and made one of them dedicated to the fax machine. Now, five staff members were required to use one line.

It is not uncommon for Trustees to have more say in the formation of ministry than those actually providing the ministries. They do this by determining who can use the facilities, what people can do with the facilities, and what equipment people can purchase to do ministry. I've seen Trustees more concerned about keeping scratches off the gym floor or the walls clean than encouraging ministry to happen.

Many churches require program staff or volunteers to ask the Trustees for the purchase of any equipment they might need to run their program. Often the Trustees say no because they do not understand the need for it, or it doesn't fit their generational paradigm. Instead of program staff or volunteers having to ask the Trustees for equipment, churches should put equipment needs in program persons' budgets and let them decide what and when to purchase.

Trustees should be concerned with providing the needed facilities for new ministries to be established. They shouldn't see their role as the protectors of the property. As the church grows, they need to delegate as many of the property decisions as possible to other people. In the small church Trustees can take care of things on a now-and-then basis, so ministries seldom suffer. But as a church grows, it often outgrows the Trustees' ability to get around to things in timely fashion. Their responsibilities outgrow their ability to handle all of the daily needs of the church in timely fashion. There are too many decisions for them to function fast enough to help Christians grow.[3]

Another long-standing tension involves the controlling tendency of Choirs or Music Directors. Most often the choir is the most controlled and closed system in a dying church. Too often, the choir director is too concerned about teaching good music regardless of whether or not it transfers the gospel to the hearts of people. No one is allowed to sing music that is different from the musical tastes of the choir or choir director. If a particular music was good enough for Jesus, it is good enough for us. God bless those musicians who love Jesus more than their music.

Origins of the Controllers

A variety of causes allow congregations to exist in captivity of the Controllers who refuse to give permission to new, innovative ministries.

Some church leaders suffer from the **small church syndrome.** This is especially true in congregations with fewer than two hundred in worship. These churches are like "Mom and Pop" stores. Mom and Dad go home together, have dinner together, and go to bed together.

34

In the Mom and Pop church, everyone knows everyone's business, and everyone goes to everything. Therefore, it is imperative that everything be coordinated so that everyone can be at everything. It also means that everyone should be part of every decision. In this case control is more a function of the size of the church than it is the result of dictatorial or non-trusting leadership.

Some people use **smoke screens** to control what happens. Some have figured out how to use their desire for coordination as a way to control what happens rather than to facilitate what needs to happen. After everything is coordinated, no time or energy exits to begin any new ministries. Others actually use a desire for empowerment to control what happens. They speak against their pastor's vision because it does not empower the laity. They speak in favor of consensus building because they know consensus can never be reached on most innovating ministries.

Some people **confuse ministry with making decisions,** better known as "running the church." When I ask laity to describe their spiritual journey, they give a long list of offices they have held in the church.

Some people must be in control of everything in order to be Somebody. These are the real Controllers. They enjoy being big fish in a little pond. Usually they are against anything that they do not think of first or that does not serve their personal needs. One of them probably comes to mind as you read this. Their insatiable desire for control is a natural trait for their generation since they have been in control of almost everything in society and the church. These are good individuals, who for the most part not only built their churches, but also built much of the twentieth-century world. They are the generations that brought "entitlement" to our society. As long as they live, they will consider themselves entitled to run this country and "their" church. Fortunately, only a few Controllers exist in each church. Unfortunately, they speak loudly and carry a big stick.

Some people **confuse accountability with control.** Control has more to do with restraint than accountability. Control is deciding what people can and can't do. Accountability is rendering an account of what a person has or has not already done. Control is more of a power issue. Accountability is more of an integrity issue. Effective permission-giving networks have built-in accountability systems but avoid control.

Some people **confuse uniformity for unity.** It is important to these people that everyone is the same.

Some people **confuse representative democracy** with the Body of Christ. They aren't the same. Money, power, or good looks are more important in representative democracy than the will of the people (or God). This may have been why the early church made the few decisions that it did make based on casting lots (Acts 1:26).

Some church leaders are simply **afraid of the unknown.** People who become comfortable with the present learn to live in the past. The last thing they want to do is to introduce the future into their environment.

Permission for members to act responsibly on their own on behalf of the Body of Christ threatens insecure or dictatorial pastors. Permission-giving means that the members no longer need co-dependent pastors to take care of them. Pastors whose self-worth is wrapped up in how much people need them are overwhelmed by a feeling of inadequacy. Much of the fuel for the raging insecurity among pastors has been provided by a weak understanding of the enabler model of ministry, or perhaps stems from the person who entered the ministry primarily to be a counselor.

We've lived with the sacred cow so long that it will

not be easy to "put it down." For some, it requires conversion. For others, it requires remembering our roots. Still others merely need to act on what they intuitively know. But in all cases those who worship this sacred cow know that the enemy of permission-giving churches lies within each of us. It goes to the heart of the first commandment.

Biblical history is full of examples of God setting people free. Liberation is at the heart of the scriptures. The four major stories of our Judeo-Christian history— Exodus, Exile, Resurrection, and Pentecost—are about the triumph of freedom and grace over all the Controllers.

Once again, Christians need to be set free, free from slavery and captivity to the Controllers who say no to new forms of ministry and routinely withhold permission from individuals to exercise their God-given gifts.

However, God does not just set us free from something. God frees us for something. We're set free to be the incredible creatures God created and not what the institutional church needs us to be. The role of Christian leaders is to help God's people discover their spiritual gifts and live them out on behalf of the Body of Christ. The Body of Christ is the foundation for the permission-giving church. It is the subject of the next chapter.

CHAPTER 4

THE CONNECTION AND FOUNDATION

"The human body employs a bewildering zoo of cells, none of which individually resembles the larger body . . . but always the results of [the brain's] orders depend on the local, autonomous cell."

David Brand

"Church members seem determined to maintain the belief that their church is a family of families."

Janet Fishburn

The Body of Christ is the best biblical metaphor to connect with the Quantum Age and lay the foundation for permission-giving networks. I choose this metaphor over metaphors of family or kingdom for several reasons.

First, the Body of Christ points toward clear images from our common experiences with our own bodies; such images as cooperation, community, equality, mutual trust, networks, unity (but never uniformity or conformity), and of course illness, ugliness, dysfunctionality, and deformity. For people born after 1950, the Body of Christ may also bring up images of health, pleasure, fitness and strength, comfort, and team work.[1]

Second, the Body of Christ is composed of networks and relationships that are in daily flux. New relationships are formed at will and networks emerge to fit the situation at hand. The Body of Christ, like the Quantum Age, is in constant change.

Third, Christians need to recover the continuity between body, mind, and spirit. The Augustinian paradigm in which sexuality is sinful and the body is to be endured until the soul is freed does not ring authentic. The Quantum Age allows us to be better in touch with the human body and all its parts.

Fourth, the Body of Christ metaphor downplays the chauvinistic, male-dominated models blessed by many established congregations. In the Body of Christ there is no male or female, parent or child. The metaphor also does not leave any room for racial, sexual, national, economic, or social prejudices (Galatians 3:23-28).

Fifth, family metaphors do not provide an adequate vocabulary to discuss the role of the Body of Christ in the quantum world. Images that come from a family metaphor are not what the Scriptures convey. Christians often place family before everything, even God. The scriptures make it very plain that nothing comes before our faith in God.

Family is never a priority issue in Scripture. It is mentioned only six times in the New Testament and never in relation to a

> **Family is never a priority issue in Scripture.**

congregation.[2] Family is always secondary to Christ's claim on us (Matthew 10:37). On several occasions Jesus de-emphasized the importance of family. Family obligations came behind the demands of discipleship. He put the disciples' obligations to the mission of the Kingdom before caring for dead family members (Matthew 8:22). On one occasion he even said that he came to cause divisions in the family (Matthew 10:35). But none of his statements about the family are more telling than when he said, "Whoever does the will of my Father in heaven

40

is my brother and sister and mother" (Matthew 12:46-50, Luke 8:19-21; 9:49-53; 14:26).

I like the way Janet Fishburn says it:

> Membership in the household of God presupposes a common faith in Jesus as Lord. Membership in a family may presuppose little more in common than biological kinship. There is no sociological entity that can accurately be called *the Christian home*. The family is not essential to the Christian life.[3]

Sixth, Kingdom metaphors do not provide an adequate symbol for the Quantum Age. Kingdom conveys images of power, control, rulership, conquest, hierarchy, monarchs, dictators, and win/lose situations.

Kingdom images do not have an authentic ring for many Christians in developing nations because they imply a form of imperialism that has been fostered by the church in various periods of its history. Often this is an image of the white man or the "patron." Kingdom images conjure up a chauvinistic, male-dominated culture.

Seventh, too many different interpretations of the Kingdom exist. Howard Snyder, in his book *Models of the Kingdom*, carefully describes eight various ways in which the Kingdom of God has been understood.[4]

I am not equating the Body of Christ with the institutional church. The institutional church is little more than a collection of people who have gotten together to form an institution for the purpose of achieving mutual goals. Some of

> **The Body of Christ is the best biblical metaphor to connect the Quantum Age and lay the foundation for permission-giving networks.**

the people within the institutional church make up the Body of Christ; some do not. The institutional church points to the Body of Christ and is, therefore, important. When faithful to Jesus Christ, it is the first fruits of the Kingdom of God. The institutional church should be the place where members of the Body of Christ are found. But they are not the same.

The Human Body

A basic understanding of the human body prepares us for a better understanding of the Body of Christ at work in the world.[5] As with all analogies and metaphors, it is best if we do not press the analogy any further than we need to explain reality.

The human body is a complex organism made up of a variety of different types of cells, totaling a hundred trillion in all.[6] Each type of cell works independently of other cells but always on behalf of the well-being of the entire body. Cells exist for the body, and life outside the body is hostile and deadly without being supplied an artificial environment. All types of cells do what they do automatically, based on what they were genetically engineered to do at conception. The genetic code for this engineering is called DNA.[7] This code is so precise that each cell contains within it all that is necessary to reassemble the entire person.

> **Understanding the human body helps us understand the Body of Christ.**

All of the types of cells are vital to the health of the body. If all the cells do their part, the body functions properly and is considered to be healthy. The individual fulfillment of each cell depends on the cooperation of all other cells. Through self-sacrifice, each cell shares in the ecstasy of community. Cell status is unimportant to the body. All that matters is the health of the body. If a foreign substance invades the body, the appropriate cells join together to fight the intruder on behalf of the body.

Cells communicate with each other through autonomous neuron cells (nerves), each of which functions on behalf of the entire body. Neurons are the most interesting of all cells, all twelve billion of them. Unlike other cells, they are never replaced since they contain our memory and understanding of how things work. Neurons are the wiring through which communication occurs throughout the body. Each neuron decides not only what signal to send to the brain, but also how it wishes to respond to the final signal the brain sends back to it.

> *The human body is a bottom-up network based on cooperation, freedom, and the common good.*

The body is a bottom-up network based on cooperation, freedom, and the common good. The brain does not direct the final movements or actions of the body as is commonly thought. Instead, signals are sent to the brain through a complicated system of cells, reflexes and conditioned reflexes, synapses (the gap between each nerve ending), and then back to the autonomous neuron. The neuron then takes action based on what it thinks is best for the body in that particular situation.

For example, if I put my hand on a hot stove, the nerve cells may abruptly tell the muscle to yank my hand off the stove since my body is not in any other form of jeopardy. But if I am in a burning car about to explode and the only way to safety is to grab hold of a red hot door handle, the neuron allows the brain to override the nerves' desire to yank my hand off the door handle and permits my hand to endure the pain.

Sometimes the brain delegates; sometimes it overrules; but always the autonomous neuron determines final outcome, always for the sake of the total organism. The brain delegates to a consistent reflex system many functions such as sneezing, swallowing, breathing, blinking, coughing, salivating. This frees up the brain for more complicated tasks.

In addition, scientists now know that in the early months of life each nerve cell connects and disconnects itself with about ten thousand other nerve cells. This may happen almost at random. By the time we are six we have about half the number of connections in our brain as we did at age two. As we learn, our nerve cells make smarter connections.

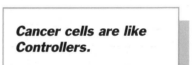

Cancer cells are like Controllers.

Mutiny and dysfunction do occur within the human body. Fat cells can become disloyal cancer cells that rob the body of room and strength. These rogue cells are just as healthy as other cells, but they are now disloyal to the body. They live for themselves, not for the body. They are the *Controllers* of the human body.

Thus, the health of the human body depends on the cooperation of autonomous cells that function on behalf of the entire organism. Each cell is totally free to do what it determines is best for the body given the stimuli that are pouring into it from all over the body as well the point of immediate concern. If cells choose to function with disregard for the body, the body is either dysfunctional or drained of its life. In the permission-giving

44

church, some cells can be treated, but some must be removed from the Body.   moo

The Body of Christ

The Body of Christ, like the human body, is a network of a variety of autonomous cells called spiritual gifts.[8] Each gift is autonomous and different, yet functions on behalf of the entire body, not the person with the gift. Individual

> *Imagine a human body where all of the parts must "get permission" before they can function.*

members of the Body of Christ find their fulfillment, not as their ministry makes them feel good but when their ministry contributes to the heath of the Body of Christ.

Imagine a human body where all of the parts must "get permission" before they can function. Or a healthy body telling a kidney or heart to quit functioning on behalf of the body. Or a lung having to get permission before it can breathe? These parts of the body function automatically without any help from the brain. So it is with most members and ministries of the Body of Christ.

The unity of the Body of Christ comes not from our sameness but from our diversity. The Body of Christ is a diversity of gifts, each one distinct and essential for the health of the Body of Christ. When each of us bless the diversity within the Body, the Body is healthy. When one of us tries to make everyone else conform to a certain path, the Body is unhealthy.

The head of the Body is Jesus Christ. It is our commitment to the Lordship of Jesus Christ as the head of this body that binds us all together. When Jesus lives in us, Christ's DNA is imprinted within us. We are made a new creature.

45

However, Christ gives each of us total freedom to make the final decision about how we live. We can be permission givers or Controllers. We can live on behalf of the common good or self. It is our choice. If we choose to bless the diversity of one another and cooperate with each other on behalf of the Body, the Body is healthy. If we choose to live for self, the Body suffers (2 Corinthians 13:5; John 14:20; 15:5; Galatians 2:20).

Paul tells us, "you are not your own" (1 Corinthians 6:19). Seeking to be like Christ means voluntarily giving up full independence. Instead we choose to live on behalf of the Body. " 'All things are lawful,' but not all things are beneficial. 'All things are lawful,' but not all things build up" (1 Corinthians 10:23). Our worth and value become intertwined with that of the Body. Our fulfillment is achieved when the Body is fulfilled.

Paul describes the Body of Christ in 1 Corinthians 12:12-20.

> For just as the body is one and has many members, and all the members of the body, though many, are one body, so it is with Christ. For in the one Spirit we were all baptized into one body—Jews or Greeks, slaves or free—and we were all made to drink of one Spirit.
>
> Indeed the body does not consist of one member but of many. If the foot would say, "Because I am not a hand, I do not belong to the body," that would not make it any less a part of the body. And if the ear would say, "Because I am not an eye, I do not belong to the body," that would not make it any less a part of the body. If the whole body were an eye, where would the hearing be? If the whole body were hearing, where would the sense of smell be? But as it is, God arranged the members in the body, each one of them, as he chose. If all were a single member, where would the body be? As it is, there are many members, yet one body.

On the contrary, it is much truer that the members of the body which seem to be weaker are necessary; and those members of the body, which we deem less honorable, on these we bestow more abundant honor, and our unseemly members come to have more abundant seemliness, whereas our seemly members have no need of it. But God has so composed the body, giving more abundant honor to that member which lacked, that there should be no division in the body, but that the members should have the same care for one another.

Now you are Christ's body, and individually members of it.

The Apostle Paul is also describing the permission-giving network. It is now our task to see how it is lived out in our congregations and denominations.

Chapter 5

PERMISSION-GIVING CHURCHES

"The more I considered Christianity, the more I have found that while it had established a rule and order, the chief aim of that order was to give room for good things to run wild."[1]

G. K. Chesterton

Rupertus Meldenius described the permission-giving church several centuries ago. To paraphrase him: "In the essentials we need unity; in the non-essentials we need freedom; but in all things we need love." It is time to describe how to develop this kind of congregation.

Permission-giving churches bend over backward to err on the side of giving permission to new ministries. They live to say yes instead of no. Making disciples, not making decisions, is their passion. Just as the human body does not try to manage everything that happens with the human body, neither do permission-giving churches. Mistakes are made, but leaders learn from their mistakes.

Every time I talk about permission-giving churches someone asks, "But how do you keep bad things from happening?" It's as if some people would rather see a church die without ever making a mistake than they would to see it thrive and make some mistakes along the way. It is almost as if we have designed our efforts around making sure *nothing* happens in order to avoid the worst possible scenario. moo

I had finished a talk on permission-giving congregations when a person came up to me and said, "All of this is well and good, but what if a group in the church were given permission to build a House for Habitat, and the people didn't wear hard hats. And what if someone on the roof dropped something on someone standing below and gave that person a concussion. And then that person was not ever able to walk again? What then? What if that person sued? What is the moral obligation of the church?"

This person went to elaborate extremes to avoid dealing with the issue of control and permission giving. Apparently, the person had searched for some rationale to negate what I was saying and justify keeping a tight reign on what the members of the congregation could and could not do. This person apparently assumes that it is wrong to give "too much" permission to new ministries. By starting with such anxiety, this person simply cannot comprehend the concept of the permission-giving church.

Permission-giving churches require a new mind-set that is comfortable with the fundamental paradox of the Quantum Age—loosely knit networks and high levels of synergy. Networks and synergy are accomplished because each congregation is clear about its values and mission, and also gives permission for each person to live out those values and mission through the exercise of their spiritual gifts.

KEY ELEMENTS

♦ *Trust*
♦ *Common mission*
♦ *Freedom*
♦ *Autonomous decision making*
♦ *Decentralization*
♦ *Networks*
♦ *Collaborative Individuals/Teams.*

All of the various ministries learn to handle themselves as autonomous units as well as to network and collaborate with other groups or individuals within or outside of the congregation or denomination. There is a deep commitment to the competency of the individual's spiritual gifts as well as the need for collaboration between alliances and individuals.

Trust and love are at the heart of permission-giving churches. Love lets go and permits the other to stretch his or her wings. Trust operates on mutual respect. Grace abounds in permission-giving churches.

The Basics of Permission-Giving Churches

Permission-giving churches believe that the role of God's people is to minister to people, in the world, every day of the week, by living out their spiritual gifts instead of running the church by sitting on committees and making decisions about what can or cannot be done.

Ministry happens when people discover their spiritual gifts instead of fulfilling roles or tasks the institution requires done. Instead of asking people to serve based on the need of the institutional church, these churches ask people, "What gifts do you bring to the Body of Christ, and what do you need from the Body to help you exercise them? Tell us and we'll equip you to use them." They view each person as a unique individual who brings wonderful gifts that the institutional church may or may not have need of at the moment but that will bring fulfillment to the Body of Christ. They

> *Permission-giving churches avoid asking people to serve on committees.*

51

want to know what spiritual gift each person brings to the Body of Christ. (Spiritual gifts are discussed in the next chapter.)

These churches help people get in touch with who they are and how God put them together. They know people blossom and seldom burn out when they begin to use their skills on behalf of the Body of Christ. They seek to help people who have no experience in the church find a place of service based on their spiritual gifts.

Permission-giving churches encourage autonomous, on-the-spot decision-making by collaborative individuals and self-organizing teams.[2] Decisions are delegated to the person closest to the ministry. Remember how the human body functions with the brain delegating the final decisions to the neurons closest to the muscles? These churches encourage the Body of Christ to function the same way. They encourage the people engaged in the ministry to make as many of the decisions as possible about how to carry out the ministry.

An image from sports may help. In football, often a coach calls the plays and the team runs the play. This is a hierarchial, decision-making sport. Permission-giving churches are more like a soccer or a basketball team. All of the players understand the game plan, but on the playing field or court, it is up to each player to make split-second decisions as to what to do. The coach has trained them and given them a game plan, but each of them is free to make decisions as the ball is moved up and down the field or court.

> **Any time,
> Any place,
> By anyone,
> no matter
> what.**

People are encouraged to begin new ministries without having to jump through a maze of decision-

52

making committees. Self-organizing Ministry Teams are one of the primary forms of ministry in the permission-giving church. Teams are discussed in chapter 9.

Permission-giving churches encourage ministry to be delivered any time, any place, by anyone, no matter what. People should not have to wait for the church to respond when they are hurting. Time is an asset instead of a limitation in the new economy of the twenty-first century. The faster a congregation can bring healing to a person's life, the healthier it will be.

Remember the last time you waited in a long line? Did you thank God for the opportu- **moo** nity to stop and rest in that line? The shorter the time lag between discovering a spiritual need and putting it into an actual ministry, the more effective the church will be in the Quantum Age. This is true for needs within the Body of Christ and in the outside community.

Two practices help shorten the time lag. (1) Don't give new ministries to existing committees to implement. They have a history of rejecting new ideas. Instead, give the implementation of the new ministry to a new, short-term Ministry Team composed of people who have a vested interest in the success of the particular ministry. (2) Avoid taking a vote on new ministries whenever possible. Bless diversity more than uniformity, and be passionate about providing choices. Blessing diversity and encouraging members to pursue their spiritual gifts is the path to unity. They know the more a church relies on representative democracy or consensus the less likely it can equip people to be servants and stewards of the grace of God.

> **Jesus never said, "Go make decisions."**

Jesus never said, "Go make decisions." The Phar-

53

isees were the ones worried about how decisions were made. How one lived and served was all that mattered to Jesus. Ask a better question: "How can we help individuals discover their spiritual gifts and use them on behalf of the Body of Christ?"

Permission-giving churches have leaders who are secure enough to equip others for ministry and then get out of their way and let them develop their ministry even if it is not something in which they might participate.

The authority of these leaders comes from their servanthood, not their power or election. Permission-giving churches have no place for co-dependent leadership, clergy, or lay. Nor is there time for lay persons who want their pastor to be a personal chaplain. Servant leaders don't feel entitled to anything.

Permission-giving churches function around a network of collaborative individuals and teams. Vertical hierarchies are replaced with decentralized, horizontal networks that require fluid structures. The development of relationships is more important than carrying out rules and regulations.

The Body of Christ is not afraid of chaos because the autonomous gifts cooperate and communicate with each other on behalf of the entire body. Just as the human body functions on freedom and cooperation, not anarchy, so the Body of Christ functions on grace not law. The body of Christ is unhealthy when individual members function primarily on their own behalf. Such action is mutiny. The Scriptures call it sin.

> *A church orgainization's first goal is to help people grow in their faith, not to "run the church."*

Permission-giving churches do need boundaries and accountability. Permission cannot be given in a vacuum. Some circumstances call for decisions to be made.[3] Freedom of choice within certain boundaries is the basic system for order and control. In permission-giving churches guidance and accountability come from the church's Mission, Vision, and Values Statements, and a clearly defined scenario plan (these instruments are discussed in chapter 10). People are free to live out their spiritual gifts within these boundaries. Governing bodies exist primarily to provide an environment in which individual members and teams can live out their spiritual gifts on behalf of the Body of Christ. (The role of the governing body is discussed in chapter 10.)

Boundaries and accountability cannot come from rule books or procedures. No book of procedures is broad enough to avoid control. For boundaries and accountability to be effective requires clarity concerning the basic values of the congregation. These basic values define the corporate culture of the congregation. They are the compass to the future.

Permission-giving churches develop a flat organizational structure that encourages and facilitates ministry instead of coordinating or managing it. The purpose of organization is to encourage and facilitate the delivery of effective ministry by the laity on and off church property.

Throughout most of the last half of the twentieth century the role of organization has been to help church leaders manage, control, and coordinate what already exists. Organization has become an end in itself. Being appointed, nominated, or elected to serve on committees is the primary form of lay ministry. Lay people see their primary leadership role to be "running the church." They spend most of their time and energy focused on what exists within the institutional church.

The permission-giving structure is just the opposite. It is a holistic, organic, self-generating, interactive, horizontal, and chaotic network of peers, designed to deliver a unique and customized mission, in a timely and consistent manner to a target audience, any place, any time, by anyone in the organization.

Because of the organic nature of the organizational structures of the Quantum Age, there is no uniform solution to every situation. No one type of organization fits every church. This requires flexibility. (This structure is discussed in chapter 8.)

Figure 1 describes the difference between the bureaucratic churches of the past and permission-giving churches of the present day.

Figure 1

Differences between Traditional Organizations
and Permission-giving Networks

The Issue	Bureaucratic Organization	Permission-giving Network
Organizational Structure	Layered/Individual	Spider Web/Team
Job Descriptions	Narrowly Focused	Mission Statements
Staff/Key Leaders	Direct/Control	Equip/Facilitate
Leadership	Top-Down	Shared Leadership
Information Flow	Controlled/Limited	Open/Accessible
Rewards	Offices/Seniority	Team- and Skill-Based
Ministry Process	Leaders Improve	Teams Improve

Permission-giving churches bring with them a host of new problems and challenges for established churches. Where do we place our boundaries? How do we set standards? How do we ensure that more good things happen than bad things? What becomes of democracy and consensus? How do we ensure accountability? These questions require more than just the sharpening of our skills. Our task now is to describe the challenges of permission-giving churches.

CHAPTER 6

DISCOVERING OUR PLACE IN GOD'S WORLD

"Now concerning spiritual gifts, brothers and sisters, I do not want you to be uninformed."

1 Corinthians 12:1

"God seems to have deliberately set up the world in a way that leaves blanks for human beings to fill."

Barbara Wendland & Stanley Menking[1]

Nowhere is the worship of the sacred cow of control more visible than in established churches' passion for standing committees, nominations and elections to church offices, building consensus, popular vote, representative democracy, equal representation, and parliamentary procedure.

However, the church has not always had this passion. The first two centuries of congregational life were organized around the various spiritual gifts of the individual members.[2] These gifts are given by God to individual members to be used on behalf of the Body of Christ. Each member is free to use his or her gifts as God leads them. Each gift and the way it was exercised was evaluated by what Paul called the "more excellent way" of love (1 Corinthians 12:31).

No mention is made of formal offices in the early church, so members are never elected to offices. This is

59

> **Authority in the early church is not vested in the consensus of the congregation or representative form of government, or nominations or elections.**

surprising since in the typical practice of the times, clubs and associations show significant interest in rewarding people with an official office.[3]

Authority is given to those who have the spiritual gift of discerning the Spirit. These individuals have the ability to determine what is or is not authentic ministry. The gift of discernment was given to individuals, not committees or official boards. Decisions are never made by consensus.

To suggest locating authority in individuals rather than committees evokes thoughts of the "p" word—power. Many church leaders, as well as most bureaucrats, have a problem with authority being vested in individuals because they associate this with some form of abusive power. Some church leaders are

> **Power can be good or bad. It can be liberating, or it can be enslaving.**

naive enough to believe that if they do not exercise power in the church no one will. Some believe that any exercise of power by the pastor mitigates against empowering the laity. This is because they see any use of power as the powerful against the powerless. However, as Martha Ellen Stortz shows, three types of power have been identified: "power over" (a commodity, i.e., sovereignty, parental, bureaucratic), "power within" (a capability, i.e., charismatic or discerning the spirits), and "power with" (a relationship, i.e., coaction and friendship).[4]

Although it is fair to say that the judicious leader draws on all three forms of power, the permission-giving leader relies most heavily on the "power with." This is the only form of authentic power described in the Scriptures. Any legitimate use of power, even "power over," is to liberate others to live out their spiritual gifts. As we shall see in chapter 7, the permission-giving leader is a team leader who exercises primarily "power within."

Authority can be good or bad, even though no one has authority unless it is given to them by another. Any abusive response to the authority one might give to another is a misuse of power. Authentic power and authority of any kind are always on behalf of the common good, i.e., the Body of Christ. When people in authority are mentioned in the Scriptures it is because of some benefit they brought to the community, not how much power they had over others. Their authority had to do with the way they functioned instead of the office they held. The emphasis was on servanthood, not election (1 Thessalonians 5:12).[5]

Distinct roles did not begin to become formalized until after the turn of the century. By the third and fourth centuries, spiritual gifts were replaced with "offices," and soon spiritual gifts were considered the domain of the clergy. Much of the New Testament understanding of ecclesia was lost during the Constantinian era.[6]

Established Protestants carried the process even further. Church offices were supplemented with bureaucracies punctuated by multi-

> *Assigning the spiritual gift of discernment to a group process, rather than to individuals, marked a major turning point in our worship of the sacred cow.*

ple standing committees and representative government. The gift of discerning the spirits, instead of being vested in individuals, was vested in committees, boards, and agencies. Consensus became more important than discernment. Establishing vision or understanding God's will became the task of a group or a process.

The fractious, egocentric spirit identified by Paul remains active today, except the resolution offered today is not one of love but rather of endless rounds of church meetings, popular vote, and representative government. Established churches assume that the discerning of the Spirit can be experienced through layers of government, due process, and popular vote. Trust, personal initiative, spontaneity, and the movement of the Spirit are verbally praised in Scripture, but structurally and programmatically discouraged by democratic parties in prayer.

Established churches are so addicted to group process and consensus building they don't encourage individuals to exercise their God-given gifts on behalf of the body of Christ. Instead, we deny our God-given personalities and uniqueness. We insist on conformity to rules and regulations. We stifle the creativity of the Spirit. Permission-giving churches are discovering the foolishness of committee work, and the importance of spiritual gifts. **moo**

Several passages of scripture give us direction at this point: Romans, 1 Corinthians 12, Ephesians 4:11-12 and 1 Peter. If you aren't familiar with this material, stop and read the texts before continuing. In these passages we learn that the Body of Christ is a collection of gifts that are as diverse as the cells within the human body. Everyone is valued because of what they can contribute to the good of the Body of Christ. Only one thing is required of each person—loyalty to the Head, Jesus Christ. Christians are held together in the Body by the

Lordship of Jesus Christ. In a sense Jesus Christ infuses us with divine DNA.

The results of emphasizing spiritual gifts instead of the traditional method of nominating people to offices brings a new vitality to a congregation. When people discover how God created them to function within the Body, the church comes alive with ministry to people rather than going to endless rounds of meetings.

What Are Spiritual Gifts?

Spiritual gifts are those special dormant spiritual abilities (Matthew 25:14-28), given to us at birth (Genesis 2:7), brought to life by the Holy Spirit in conversion (1 Corinthians 12:7, 11; 1 Peter 4:10) for the specific purpose (1 Corinthians 12:18, 28; Ephesians 4:11; Romans 12:6) of fulfilling the Body of Christ (1 Corinthians 12:27; 14:12; 1 Peter 4:10).

The scriptures are not clear as to how many spiritual gifts exist or if the number is limited only to what we see in the scriptures. Some believe that some of the gifts such as apostleship, tongues, and interpretation were relevant only to the early church. Others believe that some of the gifts, such as exorcism, healing, and miracles, are no longer valid because of advancement in our knowledge of healing and exorcism. In all cases, Paul allowed Christ and the Spirit to determine which gifts should be given at any one time or place.

My experience with spiritual gift retreats has caused me to de-emphasize such gifts as tongues, interpretation, celibacy, martyrdom, healing, and miracles. Including these valid gifts only causes

> **A list of spiritual gifts and their definiton is found in Apppendix 1.**

suspicious individuals either to dismiss any discussion of spiritual gifts or to become so curious about these spectacular gifts that they miss the rest.

The Scriptures are not clear about when God gives spiritual gifts to us: some think when a person becomes a Christian; others think when a person receives the Holy Spirit; I think at birth. None of these origins can be proved or disproved in Scripture. A person may have more than one gift, and the gifts may not be permanent but may change according to God's needs. The gifts are enhanced as they are used (Romans 12:6).

The foundation for spiritual gifts is the belief that God gives to every human being certain gifts that, when used properly, allow the Body of Christ to fulfill its role and the

> *The scriptures are clear about the importance of Christians living out their God-given gift.*

individual to develop into the incredible creature God created her or him to be. These gifts are primarily for building up the Body of Christ, and secondarily the individual.

The Scriptures are also clear that ministry belongs to individuals, not institutions. The Body of Christ is too diverse for congregations to have a ministry. Only when the diverse parts of the Body are freed to develop their God-given ministries can the Body be built up.

Spiritual gifts are not to be confused with natural talents. Natural talents are the skills we develop to accomplish something; a spiritual gift is what God does through us to accomplish something. A person's spiritual gift may determine how they use their talent. For example, singing is a talent, not a spiritual gift. Some people use their singing voice as an opportunity to spread the gospel. Others use it simply to teach music in a church setting. The difference is the exercise of a spiritual gift. The Body is best served when people exercise their spiritual gifts rather than their natural talents.

Spiritual gifts are not to be confused with the fruits of the Spirit found in Galatians. The fruits of the Spirit (love, joy, peace, patience, kindness, goodness, faithfulness, gentleness, self-control—Galatians 5:22-23) are given to every Christian, but every Christian does not have the same spiritual gift.

Why Use Spiritual Gifts?

The Scriptures give us several reasons why discovering and using our spiritual gifts are essential. It is God's will that every Christian discover and use her or his spiritual gifts (1 Corinthians 12:1). We will be held accountable to God for how we use them (1 Peter 4:10). Spiritual gifts are one way God accomplishes much of what God does in this

> "Running the church, instead of exercising their spiritual gifts, is the primary reason lay people never have time to minister to one another and the world."

world through the church (Romans 12:2-8; 1 Corinthians 12:7, 14:26). Individual Christians are not fulfilled until they discover and use their spiritual gifts (Romans 12:1-2, 6; John 15:8, 10-11; Ephesians 4:11-15). Unity is accomplished when people find their place in the Body of Christ (Ephesians 4:13). God will be glorified (1 Peter 4:11). So every Christian can minister to one another within the Body of Christ (1 Corinthians 12:7; 1 Peter 4:10).

Accomplishing the mission of the church is the primary reason for discovering spiritual gifts. "Running the church," instead of exercising their spiritual gifts, is the primary reason lay people never have time to minister to one another and the world, and why constructive biblical and theological issues seldom occupy the agendas of church or denominational meetings. They spend all of their time running the organization.

Avoiding burnout is yet another reason for emphasizing spiritual gifts. Taking care of business is why so many people find working in the church boring and time-consuming. It is also why so many people burn out on "church work." People who are equipped to use their spiritual gifts don't burn out easily or become demoralized because they are so energized by using them.

Another reason to discover spiritual gifts is that they are a great leveler of persons in the church. Just as each part of the Body of Christ is equal, so each spiritual gift is equal. Paul says "The weaker [parts] are indispensable" (1 Corinthians 12:22). Each gift is needed equally by the Body. No gift is greater than another. The quality of ministry goes up when people are encouraged to use their spiritual gifts. People are allowed to do what they do best and, therefore, the overall quality of ministry improves.

Finally, several negative things happen as a result of not discovering and using spiritual gifts. (1) The Body of Christ is never complete because many of God's gifts are overlooked. (2) Basic ministries, such as social justice, evangelism, and mercy are seldom carried out because many of the faithful few are nominated to hold an office. (3) The ministry of the church is limited to a few members who rotate around a few offices, which leads to an inactive, uninvolved membership and an overworked minority. (4) The majority of the members are dissatisfied with their life in the Christian faith. (5) The church experiences an overdependence on programs instead of spiritual growth.

A New Mind-set Is Needed

Most churches have to adopt a new mind-set before using spiritual gifts. This new mind-set includes the following changes in attitude.

Freedom, grace, and trust are more important than control and approval. Each member is free to exercise his or her spiritual gifts without having to seek someone's approval or wade through reams of paperwork. When individuals are free to exercise their spiritual gifts, decision-making, approval-giving, and standing committees are relatively unimportant. They become distant remnants of a controlling environment.

Exercising spiritual gifts is more biblical and effective than representative democracy. Only a select few attain their potential through representative democracy. Ordinary people seldom do. Democracy was never God's plan.

Discernment of God's will for the Body of Christ is more the domain of individuals than committees. Permission-giving churches are more concerned about each person finding his or her distinct ministry and place within the Body than with the health of the Body. If each part is whole, the Body will be whole. This means that accountability systems are more important than the checks and balances of the controlled environment.

Servanthood is more important than holding an office or sitting on a committee. The goal of spiritual gifts is servanthood. Permission-giving churches put a high premium on the servant positions instead of applauding the service of those who stand in the limelight and exercise power. Authority comes from how a person serves others. Those who make the few decisions that have to be made are those who serve others.

Servants exercise their spiritual gifts because of a gratitude in their heart for what Jesus Christ has done in their lives. Servants don't feel it is their duty to help the institutional church or to "put in their time" or "pay their dues." They exercise their spiritual gifts because they want to, because they receive incredible amounts of fulfillment, and most of all, because they realize that they are contributing to the building up of the Body of Christ. They are doing their part in furthering the kingdom of God, and therefore, they are becoming more mature in their faith and more skilled in their personal ministry.

Ministry is understood to be helping people instead of running the church. Running the church and making decisions is ministry only for those who have the gift of discernment. Ministry is about living out one's faith. Church business seldom has anything to do with faith in God's work.

Instead of church leaders asking people to fill predetermined positions or programs, individuals are asked, "What gifts do you bring to the Body of Christ that, if we equip you to use them, the Body of Christ will be more whole and so will you?" This question is in contrast to the traditional "Time and Talent" survey that lists the various committees and ministries the institutional church offers and then asks the people to fill it out based on what they would like to do. That is a top-down, hierarchical model that predetermines the ministries in which a member can become involved. It assumes people have had some experience in the church and understand the various committees or opportunities. People normally fill it out based on what they have done in the past, not what they want to do. The farther we go into the twenty-first century, the less people will have any experience with "working in a church."

The laity do most of the pastoral ministries and taking care of one anther, not the pastor. In this model the pastor is expected to equip the laity to do ministry. moo

Instead of rotating from one church office to another throughout their lifetime, laity dig deep into one area of the church and they find someone to mentor as their replacement. Thus, there is always someone to replace everyone.

Programs develop from the bottom up and the side in, instead of from the top down. Church leaders do not attempt to "involve" everyone in the "work of the church." Instead, they spend time finding out where people are in their spiritual journey and work with them at their point of need rather than the need of the church. This way, people grow spiritually instead of just getting involved in activities.

Spiritual Gift Inventories

Spiritual gift inventories (not tests) are basic in permission-giving churches. People are encouraged to fill out a set of questions designed to point them in the direction of their spiritual gifts. Usually, laity are trained to help individuals decipher the results of the inventory and explore how to match up their gifts with the ministries of the congregation or to decide what new ministry they might want to start.

A variety of inventories exist. Which one a church uses depends on such things as how long a person wants to spend discovering their spiritual gifts and the theology of the congregation. Some inventories are as short as five minutes,[7] some two

> *Take time to explore several of the available versions.*

hours, and some as long as six hours.[8] Some inventories are conservative[9], some are middle-of-the-road and do not include the more controversial gifts such as tongues.[10] Almost every major denomination now has its own version of inventories. You'll find one that suits your style of ministry and brings out the best in those with whom you serve.

An ancient Hindu proverb says that at one time all people thought they were divine. So Brahma decided to hide the gift of divinity. But where would he hide it? One said, "Hide it on the highest mountain." But Brahma said, "No, some day people will climb the highest mountain." Some said, "Hide it in the depths of the sea." But Brahma said, "No, some day people will plumb the depths of the sea." "Anyone else have a suggestion?" he asked. All were silent. Then Brahma had an idea: "We will hide it within each human. They will never think to look there."

Permission-giving churches encourage each person to look within to discover their gifts for the purpose of sharing those gifts with the Body of Christ. "So with yourselves; since you are eager for spiritual gifts, strive to excel in them for building up the church" (1 Corinthians 14:12).

Leadership in permission-giving churches takes on a fundamentally different role than in a traditional mainline church. We must now examine this new kind of leader.

CHAPTER 7

PERMISSION-GIVING LEADERS

"To manage is to control. To lead is to liberate."

Harrison Owen

Over the last decade more books have appeared on the subject of leadership than in any other period of time in North America. A whole new leadership industry has emerged. Why the sudden fuss over leadership?

In the mechanical, Industrial Age, organizations could succeed merely by doing more of or improving what they were already doing. Hierarchy and bureaucracy substituted adequately for leadership. When the Quantum Age emerged and the churched culture disappeared, merely doing better what churches once did no longer made disciples. Established Protestants were faced with a leadership crisis.[1]

Random, episodic, and discontinuous change requires a different kind of leadership than established church leaders are accustomed to giving. This new leadership is so different that I tried to find a better word than "leader," but I couldn't.   **moo**

In many ways the term "leader" is becoming meaningless and in some ways it is becoming more important. In permission-giving churches, leaders must "follow" the directions of those gifted in areas where the "leader" is deficient. Followers often "lead" as they exercise on-the-spot decision-making (see chapter 9). The will and ability of leaders to delegate responsibility and authority to where the knowledge resides is crucial in the quantum world. Therefore, leaders both "lead" and "follow" in permission-giving churches.[2]

This dual role of leadership requires highly balanced people as leaders. On one hand today's leaders must be self-differentiated. Murry Bowen introduced this term to depict the ability to keep two forces in balance.[3] Self-differentiated means "being separate together." On the other hand, today's leaders are self-defined in relationship to one another. Today's leaders are always in relationship with each other, never complete in themselves. They are part of a team but also the leader of the team. At times they act within the team and other times they give direction to the team. They are a team member and a team leader.

Today's leaders focus on permission giving rather than control or managing. They are both individualistic and collaborative. They network individuals and teams through a shared vision of a preferred future. They facilitate ministry in others. They do not *give* orders, or dictate how people must operate within the organization. They cast vision that creates victory, that frees people to make on-the-spot decisions, and then get out of the way.[4]   mOO   In this role they model an open and free environment in which ordinary people are en-couraged and equipped to do extraordinary ministry. Their passion is to develop other leaders who will develop other leaders.

Permission-giving leaders believe that everyone can be a leader in the area of their spiritual gift. All some people need is a

> **Permission-giving leaders identify, recruit, and equip people to use their spiritual gifts on behalf of the Body of Christ. They do not do ministry for the laity.**

role model. Others need little more than permission. Some need training in the "how to" of leadership. Permission-giving leaders develop and articulate the mission and vision of the church and create the environment in which people are free to live out their spiritual gift without having to ask permission. They see too many needs and too many possibilities to get bogged down in decision-making. They are passionate about equipping and setting people free to live out their spiritual gifts. They never see their role as taking care of people or making decisions about how to run the church.

A Conversion Adjustment

Many successful pastors from the 60s and 70s are like corporate America's middle managers. The bureaucratic, managing model worked well for them. They came up though the system, managing what existed, helping people who grew up in the church maintain the machinery, and were rewarded by a better job and a higher salary while the system began to decline.

Today, all of that has changed. In order to accomplish this type of ministry, most church leaders must go through a transformation or conversion. **moo**

This kind of radical departure reminds us of Jesus. Jesus facilitated the emerging ministry of twelve carefully chosen individuals. He focused on a few people he believed could carry on his vision of the Kingdom. He modeled and molded those disciples into permission-giving leaders. However, each disciple was free to develop his or her own vision. Mary and Martha are good examples.

If we use Jesus as our model, permission-giving

The Jesus Model
◆ Faith
◆ Vision
◆ Mentoring/Birthing
◆ Realism

leaders have four fundamental emphases: Faith, Vision, Mentoring/Birthing, and Realism.

Jesus drew his basic strength not from what he accomplished but from the fact that he knew he was loved by God no matter what he might do or not do. Because of this faith he developed a lofty ethic and a credibility beyond reproach.

Jesus had a vision of a preferred future he called the kingdom of God. This vision was the focus of his entire life. Everything about his life was tied up in this vision. This vision was what kept him focused on his mission. It was the reason he lived and died.

One aspect of Jesus' vision is seldom stressed when the good and bad points of vision are being debated. His vision encouraged people to be the incredible creatures God created them to be. His vision set people free from everything that held them in bonds. This aspect of vision is what separates religious dictators from religious liberators. Vision must free others in order to be an authentic vision.

> **To be authentic, vision must be liberating or else it isn't vision, it is manipulation.**

Jesus was a Mentor/Birther—a spiritual Midwife.[5] He was always assisting in the birth of others. He chose the Twelve to be with him so he could train them to become what God created them to be and then take his place. He spent more time with the Twelve than with the rest of society.[6]

Jesus had a realistic view of life. He knew that people were sinners. He also knew they had an incredible future because God had created them just like him. Because of that he met people where they were. Reality taught him that he could not save everyone so he didn't try. He worked with those who were open to what he was about.

Figures 2 and 3 provide a picture of these four strengths and their key elements.

Figure 2

LEADERSHIP STYLES

PERMISSION-GIVING LEADERS

FAITH	MENTOR
JESUS CHRIST	EQUIPPER
EXCELLENCE	INTERNS
INTEGRITY	LONG-TERM VIEW
COURAGE	TEAM PLAYER
VISION	**REALITY**
PRIMARY TOOL	NO ILLUSIONS
COMPASS	RESPONSIBLE
SELF-DEFINED	DETAIL
SHARED	CARE FOR SELF

(BALANCED LEADER)

HELTER-SKELTER LEADERS

FAITH	MENTOR
JESUS CHRIST	EQUIPPER
EXCELLENCE	INTERNS
INTEGRITY	LONG-TERM VIEW
COURAGE	TEAM PLAYER
	REALITY
	NO ILLUSIONS
	RESPONSIBLE
	DETAIL
	CARE FOR SELF

DO-IT-YOURSELF LEADERS

FAITH	
JESUS CHRIST	
EXCELLENCE	
INTEGRITY	
COURAGE	
VISION	**REALITY**
PRIMARY TOOL	NO ILLUSIONS
COMPASS	RESPONSIBLE
SELF-DEFINED	DETAIL
SHARED	CARE FOR SELF

DANGEROUS LEADERS

FAITH	MENTOR
JESUS CHRIST	EQUIPPER
EXCELLENCE	INTERNS
INTEGRITY	LONG-TERM VIEW
COURAGE	TEAM PLAYER
VISION	
PRIMARY TOOL	
COMPASS	
SELF-DEFINED	
SHARED	

CAREER LEADERS

	MENTOR
	EQUIPPER
	INTERNS
	LONG-TERM VIEW
	TEAM PLAYER
VISION	**REALITY**
PRIMARY TOOL	NO ILLUSIONS
COMPASS	RESPONSIBLE
SELF-DEFINED	DETAIL
SHARED	CARE FOR SELF

FRUSTRATED LEADERS

FAITH	
JESUS CHRIST	
EXCELLENCE	
INTEGRITY	
COURAGE	
VISION	
PRIMARY TOOL	
COMPASS	
SELF-DEFINED	
SHARED	

75

Figure 3

LEADERSHIP STYLES

TOUCHY-FEELY LEADERS

FAITH	MENTOR
JESUS CHRIST	EQUIPPER
EXCELLENCE	INTERNS
INTEGRITY	LONG-TERM VIEW
COURAGE	TEAM PLAYER

CONFLICTED LEADERS

VISION	REALITY
PRIMARY TOOL	NO ILLUSIONS
COMPASS	RESPONSIBLE
SELF-DEFINED	DETAIL
SHARED	CARE FOR SELF

DYSFUNCTIONAL LEADERS

	MENTOR
	EQUIPPER
	INTERNS
	LONG-TERM VIEW
	TEAM PLAYER
	REALITY
	NO ILLUSIONS
	RESPONSIBLE
	DETAIL
	CARE FOR SELF

PERSONAL CHAPLAINS

FAITH	
JESUS CHRIST	
EXCELLENCE	
INTEGRITY	
COURAGE	
	REALITY
	NO ILLUSIONS
	RESPONSIBLE
	DETAIL
	CARE FOR SELF

CRASH-AND-BURN LEADERS

	MENTOR
	EQUIPPER
	INTERNS
	LONG-TERM VIEW
	TEAM PLAYER
VISION	
PRIMARY TOOL	
COMPASS	
SELF-DEFINED	
SHARED	

CONFLICTED LEADERS

Which
of these
best
describes
your
leadership
style?

Faith

Faith is the foundation of a permission-giving leader's ministry. To "have faith" is to have experienced God through Christ in such a way as to place our total confidence in God. We are confident in what God has done and

> **Balanced leaders have an unshakable faith.**

is doing in Christ. This trust and confidence comes from our experience with God's active presence in this world through Jesus Christ.

Permission-giving leaders uncompromisingly talk about their relationship with Jesus Christ. They avoid theological hang-ups such as feeling it is necessary to distinguish between Jesus of Nazareth and the Christ of faith. They never invoke a generic God. They are clearly Christians, yet they do not feel superior to those of different beliefs. m00

To proclaim allegiance to Jesus Christ is not a negative statement that implies Christians are better than someone else. It is a statement that defines who we are and what we are about in this world. Christians are not better, just different. If we aren't proud of our difference, we have nothing to offer the world.

In a time of great change, before a person can lead others, the leader must deeply believe in what God is and can do through her or his ministry. Without this faith, the radical

> **Faith allows the leader to steadfastly and firmly move ahead when almost everyone clings to their sacred cows.**

nature and fast pace of change constantly erodes our ability to lead.

As a result of this deep faith in what God can do through human beings, permission-giving leaders strive for excellence in their spiritual lives. They are always striving to be more than they are at the moment. They do not accept the adage "I can't help it; I'm just human." Instead, they ask, "What would we be like if we were truly human?"

Personal integrity is the highest form of excellence in the permission-giving leader. Having respect for the permission-giving leader is essential or else a mentoring influence cannot be established. When the leader's values are obvious, the actions instill confidence in those who are being mentored by the leader. Today's leaders take John 14:12 seriously. "Very truly, I tell you, the one who believes in me will also do the works that I do and, in fact, will do greater works than these, because I am going to the Father."

Courage and certainty spring from faith. We know how God will act in the future based on what God has done in the past. The Scriptures provide us an adequate picture of God's work among us. This certainty goes beyond reason or reality. Faith gives the leader the certainty, courage, and perseverance to hold on to the vision with confidence when everyone else is skeptical. Faith allows a leader to experience tremendous controversy without crumbling or backpedaling, to exert enormous amounts of energy without burning out, to take unusual amounts of risk with confidence, or to experience large doses of isolation before the vision becomes a shared vision.

Because of faith, permission-giving leaders do not see themselves as professionals. They do not lead because they are professionals. They lead because God has called them, and they have no other choice.[7] They do not have a job or profession. It is not something one

78

does for money, honor, or prestige. Permission-giving leaders mentor because that is what God wants them to do. They will lead whether or not they are paid well or respected by their peers.   mOO

Vision

Vision is an over-used and underesti-mated concept. Too often it is portrayed as a bigger-than-life idea that changes as the situation changes. For many, vision is synonymous with strategy. Others see vision as little more than motivating others to do what one wants them to do.

A Balanced Leader's Vision

♦ **Is Liberating**
♦ **Is Our Compass**
♦ **Is Life-Long**
♦ **Is Life-and-Death Issue**
♦ **Must Be Shared**

Vision should be reserved for much more. Vision comes out of a person's deep belief in what God is doing in this world. Vision possesses every fiber of a person's being. You don't have a choice except to follow the path to the vision. Ancient philosophers called it "pathos." My Canadian friend, Tom Bandy, calls it "the song in your heart."

In their comprehensive study of ninety-six leaders from numerous fields, W. G. Bennis and B. Nanus found that the first quality in all great leaders is vision.[8] For a congregation to be more than the sum of its parts, a people must share a vision of where they are going and how they are going to get there. Peter Drucker warns that a single-minded mission must exist to help members stay aligned as they share complex tasks.[9]

Moses, Jesus, Martin Luther, Hitler, Dietrich Bonhoeffer, Castro, Gandhi, Martin Luther King, Jr., Nelson Mandela, and Mother Teresa are examples of people possessed by vision. Their vision determined every priority of their lives. Vision is something a person is willing to die for.

Vision can be good or bad, beautiful or insane. As we peer back in history, we can document the value and worth of a vision. Perhaps the established leaders seldom develop vision because they recall the insane visions that ignited World War Two. If our birthday is before 1946, the last thing we want to do is lead people in the wrong direction. So we don't lead them anywhere.

The best living example of vision is Nelson Mandela. He was imprisoned for twenty-five years because of his vision of a free South Africa, but the vision remained constant. He probably could have gone free if he had been willing to deny the vision. But he was unable. He did not have a vision, the vision had him. Vision is most often a lifetime passion.

Vision is always liberating. Vision liberates people to be what God created them to be, not what a few people want them to be. Authentic vision always sets people free from any form of tyranny, especially the tyranny of apathy and bureaucratic paralysis. People feel the rush of the Spirit. They believe in themselves. They attempt to soar, and they aren't afraid to risk and fail. **mOO**

In a chaotic world, vision is more important than rules or policies because it gives people authentic power and spirit. It uplifts people's aspirations and compels courage beyond what is normal. It causes people to believe that they can create the future God wants them to create.

Vision is the permission-giving leader's compass that points everyone on the ship toward his or her desti-

nation. Self-generating networks go off in all directions without vision. Leaders focus on forming and communicating the vision to encourage all of the pieces of the network to collaborate with one another. Vision helps leaders get people who are very different from the leader and one another to pull together for a common purpose. It also helps the leader stay on course in the midst of conflict.

In an uncertain world, vision is more helpful than any form of planning.[10] Vision sets the broad outline for action while leaving the specific details to be worked out. If the leaders are passionate about the vision, they can adjust to change and do not feel as if the sky is falling in. A plan without vision is useless. Allow your vision to you lead you into the future, not your plans.

Vision comes from self-defined individuals, not committees. Self-defined people know who they are in relationship to the vision and the Body of Christ. Self-defined Christians know they are deeply loved by God and, therefore, are not totally dependent on others to love and need them. They do not allow the environment to dictate their actions or let others set their agenda and decide how they spend their time.   mOO

Co-dependent leaders are the opposite of self-defined leaders.[11] Co-dependent leaders lose their self-identity within the congregation. The congregation is never sure who it is or what it stands for. Congregational creativity and enthusiasm are lost. The only thing this leader can do is help the congregation to be whatever it wants to be.

> *All of the great events in Scriptures come about through God working through one person on behalf of a people—Abraham, Moses, the Judges, the Prophets, John the Baptist, Jesus, and Paul.*

Many established church leaders make the mistake of thinking that vision comes from committees. It doesn't. Ideas can be brainstormed, vision can't. The listless momentum in our churches screams for more than ideas. Any time a committee comes forth with a vision, rest assured that an individual on the committee brought the vision to the surface, and in time that vision became the committee's vision.

In every church with which I have consulted, the corporate vision of the church is tied to the personal vision of an individual. Most often that person is the pastor. The pastor usually (1) creates and lives the vision and (2) creates the environment in which the staff and lay people can live out their spiritual gifts on behalf of the Body of Christ. If the vision results in a permission-giving church, then the vision is more bottom-up than top-down.

Vision becomes a nightmare if it does not find a shared, collective home. Vision must do more than just mirror the images of an inspiring leader. It can never be a top-down mandate. It has to capture the hopes and dreams of the congregation. It must be shaped by dialogue and prayer.

Permission-giving leaders know a vision must be shared to become a reality. No one person achieves a vision. Jesus shared leadership with the Twelve. The vision becomes complete when everyone knows what *we* want to create.

One of the best discussions on shared vision is found in Peter Senge's book *The Fifth Discipline*. Senge says, "Visions spread because of a reinforcing process of increasing clarity, enthusiasm, communication, and commitment. As people talk, the vision grows clearer."[12] This shared vision in a church comes from prayer, dialogue, and hard work.

When shared, vision can become a stream of energy that permeates a congregation, provides the energy for learning new ministries, creates

> **Vision fills every corner (field) in the congregation.**

community, eliminates competition and disorganization, and gives coherence to all the diverse parts of the Body. Nearly everyone knows why they are at church and what they are going to create in the future. Everyone can be influenced by it. It fills every corner of space (field in the quantum world) in a congregation and determines what all the parts work toward.

Failure to build a shared vision is the biggest mistake that gifted leaders can make. In their desire to create something far better, they forge ahead and don't take time to foster the growing dialogue, not allowing people to shape the vision and become part of the vision.

Three main avenues for vision sharing are open to pastors and two to lay people—the pulpit, one-on-one conversations, and small groups.

Mentors/Midwives lead by equipping others to lead in the area of their spiritual gifts. Their goal is to bring out the hidden spiritual gifts and talents that lie buried within others. Peter Koestenbaum goes so far as to says, "Ethics in leadership is the commitment to make others successful."[13] Mentors/Midwives thrive on setting people free. They act as spiritual midwives, helping others give birth to the gifts within them.

> **Balanced leaders understand the importance of relationship and helping others achieve.**

When you look at someone else, what do you see? A person you can help or a person you can equip and set free? If all you see is someone to help, the probability is slim that you will be a leader in the Quantum Age, no matter how effective you might have been in the past. If you are able to see in people more than they can see in themselves,

moo   and are willing to equip them and set them free, you have the ability to be a leader in the Quantum Age.

Three things are essential to set people free. (1) People must be responsible for their actions and have the authority to make on-the-spot decisions. Leaders must be willing to get out of the way and let things happen that they do not have control over. Church leaders must be willing to give up control. (2) Mentors must not abdicate when delegating. Equipped individuals still need guidance on how to function so that the Body is whole. This guidance is achieved through Mission, Vision, and Value Statements. (3) Support, encouragement, respect, and resources are also essential. It is not enough to equip people and then not value and validate who they are and what they are doing.

Mentors/Midwives always have interns or apprentices. They are always looking for their replacement so they can go on to the next mentoring experience. The mentor's/ birther's role is always to work himself or herself out of a job.

> *Who are you mentoring or helping give birth to what God has placed inside?*

I know one mentor who never makes hospital calls alone. She always takes a lay person with her. Her goal is to bring that person to the point where he or she will make hospital visits without her. I know of another mentor who never prays for people in the hospital until they first pray (of course this does not apply when the patient

> **Compound ministry is the way to the future.**

is unconscious). If the patient does not know how to pray, the pastor asks the person to just say "thank you" and then the pastor prays. This pastor will not want to pray in place of the patient but alongside the patient. I know another pastor who always looked for a replacement during the first session of any new Bible study.

Mentors take a long-term view instead of looking for quick fixes. Mentors understand "compound ministry." They know that if they equip one person every six months and that person mentors another person who mentors another and so on, by the fifth year 512 people are equipped. They never see a ministry as something that starts and stops. They always look for the residual. They always anticipate how today's actions will effect the future of the Body and the individual.

It is always easier to do something than to equip someone else to do it. However, once you have done it yourself, if it is to be done again, you must do it again. If it needs to be done more than once, you must do it more than once. If you equip someone else to do it, it can be done twice with the same amount of effort on your part as if it were done only once.

Mentors/Midwives are team players. They share in the failures of individuals or the team. Their typical response might be, "Where did I fail to equip you?" Mentors/midwives avoid casting blame. They are always alongside each member of the team sharing in the good and the bad. This is the continuous learning experience the mentor must have in order to find fulfillment.

Realism

Permission-giving leaders face reality as it is, not as they wish it were. They are objective enough to minimize illusions. They understand that self-deception can cost them their vision. They understand their limitations

> **Balanced leaders have uncommon "common" sense.**

and surround themselves with quality in their areas of weakness. They accurately assess the magnitude of the obstacles in front of their vision. They know their ability to delegate as well as the strengths of the people with whom they minister. Realistic leaders say no to their ego and avoid a dictatorial type of leadership.   moo

Realistic leaders have an abundance of common sense. They don't try to make things complicated. Realism brings vision down to earth. Vision can become a nightmare or be so embellished that the leader can no longer separate fact from fiction. Realistic leaders are able to avoid the frustrations of people who dream pipe dreams. Instead, they are more prone toward having vision than dreams.

Realistic leaders take responsibility for their actions. They do not blame the system for the way things are or wait until things get better before they act. Instead, they live their vision now. They live the vision before it exists. Others can sense it through them before it happens.

Realistic leaders know that vision without details never goes anywhere. They devour all the information they can. They constantly monitor all of the vital systems of the church and society. They understand the demographics of their region. They have written objectives. Usually these objectives are present to remind them of their vision. Realistic leaders are not afraid of strategy.

Realism forces the leader to safeguard his or her personal health. They have a built-in time clock that says "Enough. Time out!" These leaders build in time for God, self, and family.

Leadership Blocks

The quantum world requires balanced leaders. Each of the above four traits is essential to permission-giving leadership. When one is absent, the leader is out of balance.

Figures 2 and 3 display the various styles of leadership. In every block but one, one or more of the segments is empty. The absence of one or more of the four essential traits for permission-giving leadership does not mean that particular trait is totally absent in that person. It means that the person tends not to draw on that trait as often as she or he should. As a result, the style of ministry is out of balance.

Balanced, permission-giving Leaders develop and use all four traits. One may be stronger than the others, but all four strengths are in use most of the time. When these four strengths are present in equal amounts, a person has the potential to be an exceptionally effective leader.

PERMISSION-GIVING LEADERS

FAITH	MENTOR
JESUS CHRIST	EQUIPPER
EXCELLENCE	INTERNS
INTEGRITY	LONG-TERM VIEW
COURAGE	TEAM PLAYER
VISION	REALITY
PRIMARY TOOL	NO ILLUSIONS
COMPASS	RESPONSIBLE
SELF-DEFINED	DETAIL
SHARED	CARE FOR SELF

When one of these strengths is under or overdeveloped, the leader's ability to be effective is lessened.

If you find yourself in this category, you have all the necessary ingredients to be a permission-giving leader. This does not mean that you are such a leader at the moment. Your leadership may be stifled by a bureaucratic system.   **mOO**   Give yourself permission to be a leader. Begin to model permission giving and mentor someone to do the same.

Helter-Skelter Leaders have everything except direction. They do not draw enough on vision. They deeply care about people but are unable to cast vision and give direction to the overall ministry. Therefore, no one is clear about the basic mission of the church and people go off in all directions. This is one of three primary leadership models in established churches.

HELTER-SKELTER LEADERS	
FAITH	MENTOR
JESUS CHRIST	EQUIPPER
EXCELLENCE	INTERNS
INTEGRITY	LONG-TERM VIEW
COURAGE	TEAM PLAYER
	REALITY
	NO ILLUSIONS
	RESPONSIBLE
	DETAIL
	CARE FOR SELF

If you feel deficient in this trait, consider one or more of the following:

1. Read the biographies of the great visionaries past and present. Get to know how they think and feel about reality. Three examples are the biographies of Nelson Mandela, Benjamin Franklin, and George Patton.

2. Surround yourself with people who have a vision larger than life and are willing to give themselves to making that vision a reality. These can be people you know or people you read about.

3. Gather around you people who, like yourself, dream of a better day for their church but have no idea

what the dream looks like or how to achieve it. Every church has a few people who dream of a preferred future for their community of faith. All they need is someone who is willing to dream and journey with them toward a better day.

4. For some, it will help to explore the world of puzzles, or chess, or philosophy, or something else. Leonard Sweet, Chancellor of United Seminary, says that in order to understand today's world, one must play computer games to learn how to use intuitive reasoning.[14] Attempt exercises that will expand and challenge your mind. Often the everyday strain of ministry drains us of our childish desire to know more about life.[15]

Do-It-Yourself Leaders are either lone wolves, dictatorial leaders, disorganized, or consider delegation to be an abdication of responsibility. They do not draw enough on mentoring/ midwifing skills. These leaders tend to be workaholics and sometimes are very hard to work

DO-IT-YOURSELF LEADERS

FAITH	
JESUS CHRIST	
EXCELLENCE	
INTEGRITY	
COURAGE	
VISION	REALITY
PRIMARY TOOL	NO ILLUSIONS
COMPASS	RESPONSIBLE
SELF-DEFINED	DETAIL
SHARED	CARE FOR SELF

with. They work harder and harder and get farther behind. This style of leadership worked well during the Industrial Age and while our culture was thoroughly churched.

If you feel deficient in this trait, consider one or more of the following:

1. Remember that good works can't save you. It is by grace that we all are saved. God is the center of ministry, not us. You are not a savior.

2. Practice delegation. A good book that weaves delegation into the heart of a system is Tom Peters's *Thriving on Chaos*.[16]

Delegation can be learned over a period of time. Check out your laity. Many churches have laity skilled in the art of delegation. Ask them to mentor you. Begin delegating small things to people you trust. Monitor how they are doing. Give them more responsibility as they develop.

I have found the following six types of delegating helpful in deciding how much to delegate to a person. Depending on the level of development in the person, you can use one of the following delegation styles. (1) "Check this out and give me the particulars. I'll decide." (2) "I'll review your analysis and recommendations and get back to you." (3) "You decide. Let me know your decision. Wait for my go-ahead." (4) "You decide. Notify me of your decision. If you don't hear from me by ____, implement your decision." (5) "You decide and take action. Let me know what you've done." (6) "You decide and take action. There is no need to check back with me."

3. Developing team skills is essential. Read many of the new books on team or collaborative leadership.[17]

Dangerous Leaders have a hard time separating fact from fiction. They do not draw enough on realism. They have a great passion for new ideas and know how to push those ideas through without much regard for the financial consequences or the loss of relationships. Administration is not their strength.

DANGEROUS LEADERS

FAITH	MENTOR
JESUS CHRIST	EQUIPPER
EXCELLENCE	INTERNS
INTEGRITY	LONG-TERM VIEW
COURAGE	TEAM PLAYER
VISION	
PRIMARY TOOL	
COMPASS	
SELF-DEFINED	
SHARED	

If you feel deficient in this trait, consider one or more of the following:

1. Concentrate on writing down your goals. Once this is accomplished, evaluate every action in light of these goals.

2. Learn to read financial statements and study the church's financial statement each month.

3. Use some form of diagnostic tool to help you keep informed about the progress of the church. While a pastor, each year I used "The Ministry Audit" in the back of *The Church Growth Handbook*. This instrument provided me an annual benchmark to compare the progress or decline in every area of the life of the church.

4. Take courses in business administration at a local college or university. Seek out people in the church who are strong in the business world and let them mentor you.

5. Surround yourself with lay people who are strong on common sense. This will be harder than you might think. Common sense is almost a lost strength today.

CAREER LEADERS

	MENTOR
	EQUIPPER
	INTERNS
	LONG-TERM VIEW
	TEAM PLAYER
VISION	REALITY
PRIMARY TOOL	NO ILLUSIONS
COMPASS	RESPONSIBLE
SELF-DEFINED	DETAIL
SHARED	CARE FOR SELF

Career Leaders approach everything as if it were a business. They do not draw enough on their faith. They rely too little on the faith dimension of ministry. This flaw could be attributed to the career-oriented pastor, the music director who uses the church primarily as a place to

91

teach music, or the lay person who is related only to the institutional church. Everything is approached as if it were a business. Strategies are more important than prayer. These leaders lack the spirituality to lead people through the wilderness of the unchurched society. This is one of the three primary leadership models in mainline Protestantism.

If you feel deficient in this trait, consider one or more of the following:

1. Begin or expand your own personal devotional and prayer life. Set aside a regular time daily for Bible study, prayer, and contemplation about your role in God's world.

2. Find a small group of people who desire to deepen their spiritual life and develop regular times together for Bible study and prayer. At the same time, attach yourself to a person you consider to have an abundance of faith.

3. Find an accountability partner and allow him or her to monitor your spiritual development.

4. In some cases it may be as simple as rediscovering the power of your call or disciplining your prayer life. Often, we drift so far from our roots that we forget how we first felt when God came into our lives.

5. Sometimes a spiritual formation retreat allows you the time to focus on your relationship with God without the needs of others constantly clamoring for your attention.

Figures 6 through 11 represent highly ineffective people. In each case some form of clinical help may be necessary.

Frustrated Leaders have a deep passion for building a great church but lack the relational and informational skills to accomplish much of anything. Coupled with not being able to tell fact from fiction and not forming solid relationships with others, they seldom experience fulfillment and neither do those around

FRUSTRATED LEADERS

FAITH JESUS CHRIST EXCELLENCE INTEGRITY COURAGE	
VISION PRIMARY TOOL COMPASS SELF-DEFINED SHARED	

them. They do not draw enough on mentoring/midwifery and realism.

If you feel deficient in these traits, consider everything recommended for the do-it-yourself leader and the dangerous leader (see Chapter 7).

Touchy-Feely Leaders put relationships above everything else. They do not draw enough on vision and reaslim. It is impossible for them to be leaders for fear of upsetting someone. They border on being dysfunctional.

TOUCHY-FEELY LEADERS

FAITH JESUS CHRIST EXCELLENCE INTEGRITY COURAGE	MENTOR EQUIPPER INTERNS LONG-TERM VIEW TEAM PLAYER

If you feel deficient in these traits, consider everything recommended for the helter-skelter and dangerous leader (see Chapter 7).

Conflicted Leaders are torn between the dream and the reality. They do not draw enough on faith and mentoring/birthing. They miss much of the joy of ministry. Relationships are tenuous and far between. They tend to chew up people and spit them out in pursuit of their goals. Often the church is nothing more than a vehicle to promote a singular cause. Although the cause may be worth pursuing, people not affected or inspired by the cause are often ignored or neglected.

If you feel deficient in these traits, consider everything recommended for the do-it-yourself leader and the career leader (see Chapter 7).

CONFLICTED LEADERS

VISION PRIMARY TOOL COMPASS SELF-DEFINED SHARED	REALITY NO ILLUSIONS RESPONSIBLE DETAIL CARE FOR SELF

Dysfunctional Leaders receive all of their self-worth from the approval of others. They do not draw enough on faith and vision. They seldom have a personal agenda and nearly always do what others want done. They try to be all things to all people.

If you feel deficient in these traits, consider the following:

DYSFUNCTIONAL LEADERS

	MENTOR EQUIPPER INTERNS LONG-TERM VIEW TEAM PLAYER
	REALITY NO ILLUSIONS RESPONSIBLE DETAIL CARE FOR SELF

1. Everything recommended for the helter-skelter leader and the career leader (see Chapter 7).

2. Remember, God loves you just as you are; you do not have to prove anything to God, and you do not need anyone's approval to be a complete human being.

3. Begin exploring with a professional counselor

why you have this need for others to need and like you.

Personal Chaplain Leaders think ministry is taking care of people. They do not draw enough on mentoring/birthing and vision. They genuinely care about people but do not have any desire to equip them to care for themselves and others. However, they are seldom dysfunctional. This is one of the three primary leadership models in mainline Protestantism.

If you feel deficient in these traits, consider everything recommended for the helter-skelter leader and the do-it-yourself leader (see Chapter 7).

PERSONAL CHAPLAINS

FAITH	
JESUS CHRIST	
EXCELLENCE	
INTEGRITY	
COURAGE	
	REALITY
	NO ILLUSIONS
	RESPONSIBLE
	DETAIL
	CARE FOR SELF

Crash-and-Burn Leaders do great things for a period of time and then everything comes apart. They do not draw enough on faith and realism. They are great with people. Their vision inspires a great following. But the lack of realism brings enormous pain to those who follow. The lack of faith leaves these leaders drained from the constant effort to inspire others.

If you feel deficient in these traits then consider everything recommended for the dangerous leader and the career leader (see Chapter 7).

PERMISSION GIVING LEADERS

	MENTOR
	EQUIPPER
	INTERNS
	LONG-TERM VIEW
	TEAM PLAYER
VISION	
PRIMARY TOOL	
COMPASS	
SELF-DEFINED	
SHARED	

The Leadership Question

Permission-giving leaders ask one question.

The question may be spoken in a variety of ways, but the spirit of the words conveys this message. This question

> *How am I going to use my spiritual gifts today to encourage someone else to help the Body of Christ to grow and mature tomorrow?*

leads to an-swers that undergird the deepest form of leadership.

This form of leadership encourages spiritual and emotional freedom. It does not imply control, power, coercion, or threat. Any authority it evokes is given only by consent. In the Quantum Age, leaders can no longer mount a charge to fix things.   **mOO**
Leaders can only seek to liberate and inspire.

However, leaders cannot be liberating if the system in which they live out their spiritual gifts is bureaucratic and hierarchical. Spiritual gifts do not blossom well in a controlling environment. A new form of organization is needed: the permission-giving network.

CHAPTER 8

PERMISSION-GIVING NETWORKS

"The world no longer needs the machine-like organizations bureaucracy produces."

Gifford and Elizabeth Pinchot

Permission-giving churches require an organization that encourages each individual to use his or her spiritual gifts on behalf of the Body of Christ without going through a maze of committees to get approval. Networking is the foundation of this organization.

However, maintaining the bureaucracy has received the lion's share of denominational leaders' attention over the past few decades. Control, power, hierarchy, career, professionalism, status, prestige, ladder climbing, and resolutions have been our focus. **mOO**

Throughout the Industrial Age, the structure of most organizations,

R.I.P.

BUREAUCRACY

1890-1999

including Protestant denominations, has been a hierarchy of boxes and lines stacked and drawn on descending levels of responsibility, accountability, control, and authority. The levels ranged from "upper" to "middle" to "lower." Information traveled up and down the levels of the flow chart with little if any lateral or cross pollination of ideas or information. Often the primary goal of personnel is to "climb the [hierarchical] ladder." The higher one goes, the more one is paid and respected. Often the "glass ceiling" keeps women and minorities out of "upper" management. The end result of this model is called bureaucracy.

As long as society remained stable and sympathetic to Christianity, this method of organization kept churches and denominations fairly well organized. However, when society became unstable and its attitude toward Christianity began to change, this method of organization became a major liability.

Most forms of bureaucracy will not survive the first half of the twenty-first century. As the machine-like Industrial Age fades away, a new economy driven by microprocessors instead of combustible engines requires organizations to be able to process information (as opposed to storing information) and constantly learn. The paradoxical world of quantum physics and the multi-layered world of the microprocessor produces problems too complex and demanding for bureaucracy for the following reasons.

Bureaucracies are founded on a hierarchical structure that fosters dominance and submission, which produces distrust and fear of telling the truth.[1] Any one who suggests an alternative to the present policy or procedure is often ignored, or demoted. Bureaucrats look for one right answer and then avoid conflict by suppressing all other ways of thinking. Bureaucracy has a long history of shooting the messenger and discouraging communication of the whole truth. Truth is discouraged when it threatens the status quo. Often, bureaucrats know what they need to do to get their denomination on track again, but they don't make any attempt to do so because they know what happens to people who question the status quo.   moo

Bureaucracy consists of relationships of dominance and submission up and down a chain of command that often discriminates against women and races. Power and accountability are more important than ministry and responsibility. New ideas can be stopped any place along the chain. Information seldom flows horizontally and often a

Bureaucratic Weaknesses
♦ *Simplistic Orientation*
♦ *Hierarchical*
♦ *Power, Dominance, Submission*
♦ *Fixed Relationships*
♦ *No One in Charge*
♦ *Reductionist Thinking*
♦ *Organized to Manage*
♦ *Organization*

sizable piece of information can be withheld from most of the people in the organization.

Bureaucracy has a fixed set of relationships and solutions for processing problems, which causes it to be ineffective in a complex, diverse world of choices.[2] Everyone does one job and does it one way.

Bureaucracy finds change very difficult because almost no one has the power to make substantial changes. Everyone waits on everyone else because no one wants to be out of step with the status quo. In such a system it is easy for one to blame his or her lack of action on someone else's lack of action. Today's fast pace of change renders bureaucracy helpless.

Bureaucracy embraces reductionist thinking as its

fundamental principle of organization. Everything is divided into pieces so that each piece of the organization is separate from and has little or nothing to do with the whole. The "thinking part" of bureaucracy is seldom aware of what the "doing part" has observed. The result is that there is seldom any cross-learning within the organization. Almost every effective organization today is organized around the relationship of the parts to the whole. The growing demand for the swift flow and processing of information and learning cannot be responded to by bureaucracy.

Over time, bureaucrats become more interested in managing the organization than in carrying out the business of the organization. Bureaucrats are more concerned with ensuring the life of the denomination than assuring the denomination has an authentic ministry and reason for existence. Jesus had a series of hard words for those who care more for form than they do for substance (Matthew 15:2-3, 6; Mark 7:5, 8, 13). **mOO**

However, even though the Industrial Age is over and bureaucracies are no longer effective, most organizations still are formed around some type of bureaucracy. Denominations are no exception. The organizational structures of established denominations and churches remain much the same as they have been for two hundred years, even though almost every denomination has undergone some attempt at organizational change in the past thirty years. The boxes and lines defining the hierarchy and linear operations may have been moved around, but the way in which the organizations function and think has changed very little.

According to Stanley Davis in *Future Perfect*, it is not unusual for organizational structures to be the last change in the evolutionary chain.[3] So, it is not unusual for denominations to want to hold on to their bureaucracy.

However, people born after 1950 are creating a new way of organizing through their emphasis on relationships and computers. Churches that want to reach them must design organizations that emphasize relationships and networks instead of a chain of command, stress men-

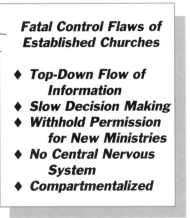

Fatal Control Flaws of Established Churches

♦ **Top-Down Flow of Information**
♦ **Slow Decision Making**
♦ **Withhold Permission for New Ministries**
♦ **No Central Nervous System**
♦ **Compartmentalized**

toring and self-organizing instead of bossing, are comfortable with complexity and paradox instead of the status quo, and see time, space, and matter as resources instead of constraints. **mOO**

The more intent a church or denomination is on reaching the unchurched in the twenty-first century the more it will abandon bureaucracy in search of a new method of organizing for ministry. Solid clues are already emerging that give us insight to the effective organizations of the future.

The Permission-giving Network

Relationships and networks are more important than a chain of command.

Permission-giving churches are an ever-changing web of networks that connect together people and information so that communication and decision making can occur quickly and directly no matter how far removed people are geographically or organizationally.

> **Reciprocity is essential to effective networks.**

Networking creates an organizational structure that relates all of the parts to the whole and allows for communication between every part, at every level, at every point of need, whenever the need may arise, in the shortest time possible.

An electronic bulletin board service (BBS) is an excellent example of a network. Bulletin board services are found on a number of on-line services such as Compuserve, Prodigy, or America On Line. Anyone with access to an on-line service can log on anytime, anyplace, with anyone if the phone line is not too busy. No one gives or withholds permission. No one is forced to pay attention or to respond. No one is coerced to do anything. Plugging into the network is potentially beneficial to everyone on the network, not just the one sending the message seeking a response.[4]

Permission-giving networks are open-ended systems. These open systems are in constant flux, always poised for reordering, capable of endless transformation. Some people go so far as to talk about "organic organizations," more biological than mechanical. They speak of networks as living, open space systems capable of thinking, self-renewal, and community.[5]

This organic mode of social organization is more biologically adaptive, more efficient, and more "conscious" than the hierarchical structures of modern civilization. The network is plastic, flexible. In effect, each member is the center of the network.

Networks are cooperative, not competitive. They are true grass roots: self-generating, self-organizing, sometimes even self-destructing. They represent a process, a journey, not a frozen structure.[6]

On-the-spot decision making is expected in open-ended systems. Effective organizations do not include vertical chains of command or flow of information. Top-down management and flow of information is used only in dire emergencies. Candid and full disclosure of all information is essential if each part of the Body is to grow and learn and if the Body itself is to be whole. The goal is to encourage decisions to be made anytime, anyplace, by anyone.

> *Information flows in all directions and is available to anyone, anytime, under any circumstance.*

Instead of levels, boxes, or lines, networks more closely resemble the structure of the human cells or atom-like structures. Networks can be compared to a spider's web that begins with a carefully spun single strand of silk. In time, so many strands of silk weave back and forth, up and down, that it is impossible to see the single strand anymore. All one can see is a solid web blanketing the area.

Networks do not worry much about span of control because in some way all of the parts are connected to each other. If organizations are viewed as machines, control is important. If organizations are viewed as living organisms, imposing any form of control impedes the process. Control in the new organization is replaced with interaction between the parts of the network on behalf of the whole.

Networks may or may not have any formal contiguous or recognizable configuration. They can change from day to day depending

> *Control is not important in networks.*

103

> *A copy of the Ministry Tree is in Appendix 3.*

on who comes into relationship with another in the network. New people mean new opportunities for growth and ministry. The organization of the future is one that can change according to the needs of those involved with the ministry of the church.

Colonial Hills had the "Ministry Tree" network. One end of the organizational chart resembled a tree. Like all trees, new leaves constantly emerged and old leaves dropped off. The actual shape of the organizational chart changed weekly and sometimes daily. People were free to plug in to or abandon the Ministry Tree anytime they chose. They could jump from limb to limb or leaf to leaf anytime they felt their spiritual journey would be helped or they could do more for the Body. However, remember that just because it worked for Colonial Hills does not mean it will work for your church, because the organizational structure must be designed to support your specific goals and ministries.

> *If you can diagram it, it probably won't work.*

No one organizational structure will work in the twenty-first century, either for congregations or denominations. There is no "right" form of organization. It is becoming increasingly difficult to develop organizational or informational flow charts. As soon as one is developed, the needs of the organization change. The easier it is to diagram an organization, the more ineffective the organization will be. The organization of the twenty-first century is too complex and changes too often. If an organizational chart

104

has vertical lines that connect boxes, it is definitely a dinosaur. If a structure clearly makes some people inferior to others, it does not understand the importance of networks. **moO**

However, all effective church structures will have one thing in common—they will be specifically designed to facilitate the particular mission of the congregation, not the denomination.

In changing times like these, it is best if an organization is designed to facilitate new ministries instead of sustaining long-term ministries or controlling what happens.

> **Does your organization encourage and facilitate new ministries?**

Therefore, structure should develop as a natural expression of the mission of the congregation or denomination.[7] The mission and the culture determine the form of the organization. "Organizational structure is like a pair of shoes. You fit the shoes to the feet; you don't make the feet fit the shoes."[8] If the leaders of the church own the mission, the structure will happen to make the mission come true.

Open-ended systems don't have much use for job descriptions. The nature of work is changing so fast in network organizations they are hardly worth developing. Some are even suggesting that the "job" is an artifact whose days are numbered.[9] The job is an idea that was created in the nineteenth century to package the work that was done in growing factories and bureaucracies of the Industrial Age. Before jobs, people worked just as hard as they do now, but they worked on changing clusters of tasks, in a variety of locations, on a schedule set by the sun, weather, and the needs of that particular day. The modern job was a startling new idea.

Today, what we call the "job" is no longer needed. We are in transition from a world built on jobs to a world consisting of fields or clusters of work needing to be done. The work will be done by constantly changing teams of laity, consultants, and paid staff. More and more support help like secretaries will be part-time and do the work in their homes instead of the church office. People will be rewarded for reaching an objective rather than "doing their job."   moO

Permission-giving networks ask the following questions: Is work being done by the right people? Are the core ministries being done by our key leaders? Are laity freed up for ministry? Are the people who do the ministries in each of those categories chosen in such a way that their desires, abilities, temperaments, spiritual gifts, and assets are matched with the demands of the task? Is everyone compensated in the most appropriate way? Is everyone involved given all the available information the church has?

Instead of job descriptions, churches have to know where they are going and find the kind of people who will help them get there. If they have the right

> **Does our organization help laity and staff complete their goals?**

people, people who understand the direction, have the spiritual gifts and talents, and have access to the right information, they will find out how to get there without job descriptions.

Staff effectiveness is measured by what they are helping others to accomplish, not how many hours they are in the office. Staff need to be free to establish new networks, set their own hours and vacations, and select what ministries they want to focus on as needs arise.

The goal is that in time they learn to manage themselves for the good of the Body.

Permission-giving networks focus on personal and corporate growth. The further we go into the twenty-first century the more every

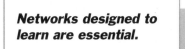

Networks designed to learn are essential.

organization is going to struggle with the limitations of their knowledge. Ministry and leadership will continue to become more complex in the Quantum Age. Needs will continue to multiply. Immaturity of all kinds will increase as technology grows faster than people's ability to assimilate. More and more intelligence will be required at every level of ministry. The only way the church can stay relevant is by interconnecting all of the brains of the organization. These are called learning networks.[10]

Learning is more important than doing. Church leaders often work harder and get farther behind until they learn new ways to accomplish old ministries. Most of the leaders I talk with tell me that they seldom distinguish between learning and doing. In the learning organization, unlike the training received in seminary, where a person studies and then does, today's leader learns while doing. Learning becomes a day-to-day experience as opposed to learning and then doing.

Learning networks adapt themselves to each problem or need through the interaction of problems, people, and resources. Members of the network organization autonomously work out their relationships. Networks continually redesign themselves to address new tasks, problems, or changing environments.

The more interconnected an organization becomes, the more ability it has to learn and grow in faith and

> **High levels of learning from Team work.**

action. The right combination of minds results in new insights and more effective ministries. Like computers, the massive parallel architecture of networks produces a high level of learning. People communicate slowly and learn slowly compared to computers, unless you have many people working and talking about the same problem all at the same time. Then high-level, fast learning is achieved.

Permission-giving networks understand chaos to be a catalyst for growth and understanding in the Quantum Age. Twentieth century organizational patterns have revolved around an effort to control the work and events experienced by an organization. Managers talked about "span of control" and "quality control."

> **Create a little chaos now and then. It is good for the soul of the church.**

Chaos was avoided at all costs. Because of our Western orientation, we tend to think of chaos as bad or wrong and order as good and right. Neither is true. Chaos and order are not opposites; they are paradoxical. They are the Yin and the Yang of growth. Yin and Yang are the Eastern way of talking about balance. We are always moving from one to the other.

Those who embrace chaos as much as order are the best prepared for life in the Quantum Age. In the Quantum Age order is found when one is immersed enough in the chaos to see the patterns of the new order emerging. Permission-giving leaders are always evaluating the emerging edges of chaos for a glimpse of the future.[11]

Bureaucrats hold to order so tightly that they are

always dealing with what was. Most church leaders will go to any lengths to avoid chaos. Often they say "no" to a good idea because something in the past

> *What we should be doing is asking, "What can we learn from this mess?"*

did not work out according to their plan. When chaos does occur, they respond by either running, hiding, seeking a quick fix, or yearning for the good old days. The real test of an organization's strength and ability to learn is how well it handles chaos.

Much is being learned today about the scientific predictability of chaos and its relationship to innovation and learning. Chaos is understood to be the catalyst of the foundations of the twenty-first century. Chaos theorists suggest that chaos not only has order and predictability but is also useful because it is through chaos that old systems are reborn.[12] Through the use of computers, we have learned that what was thought to be the random response of chaos is actually a series of beautiful patterns repeated over and over.[13] In one of the hottest debates of the twentieth century, chaos theorists are challenging the Second Law of Thermodynamics of Newtonian physics, which says all systems wind down sooner or later and die. Because of chaos, systems do not eventually wind down and die, they become reborn into a new system.

In the quantum world, real learning takes place when chaos is responded to openly and with insight. One has to have a certain amount of common sense and experience as well as intelligence to be able to see what the chaos has to offer. The point is that without chaos, there is nothing new. Harrison Owen says, "Chaos creates the differences that make a difference, through which we learn."[14]

When I talk with pastors about breakthroughs in their ministries, they often mention either the presence of chaos or new vision. Unfortunately, for many, the chaos is often the product of burnout or a nervous breakdown. Without the vision, chaos can happen and the breakthrough it creates and the reality it unveils go unnoticed.

> **The Holy Spirit has a way of moving a church beyond its comfort zone.**

One of the most vivid memories from my readings of the Acts of the Apostles is that almost every time people come in contact with the risen Christ or the Holy Spirit, chaos occurs and the church is moved out of its comfort zone. On the Day of Pentecost the disciples were scattered abroad. Saul was wrenched from his comfortable pharisee's pension to become Paul and preach the Gospel from hand-to-mouth. Ananias was killed on the spot for withholding what rightly belonged to God. Peter had to eat pork with a Gentile. God seems to work best through those chaotic moments when our world is turned upside down.

Permission-giving networks organize to facilitate and encourage relationships and the flow of information through teams and small groups. Relationships and the flow of information are the two most valuable assets of the permission-giving network. The primary question for any organization is, "How do we organize and encourage relationships and the flow of information?"[15] The sum of an organization is the sum of its parts plus the relationships between the parts.

> **The relationships between the parts is what facilitates information and learning.**

Therefore, relationships are the key leverage points for changing a system's performance. Change the relationships and the organization changes. Relationships are based on the person and his or her skills instead of the role the person has in the organization. Unlike networks, committees and church offices are based on roles, not persons or relationships. People are thrown together without any thought as to how they will connect with each other. This will not do in a world built on diversity. Teams must be built on affinity.

Permission-giving organizations exist to create the conditions in which free choices lead to the cooperation of all areas on behalf of the Body. If a problem emerges for which there appears to be more than one solution, the network organization forms a team for each solution and encourages each team to work on the same issue.[16]

Turf issues are a primary obstacle to networking a congregation.

The flow of information is in all directions. When a person's hunger for growth and knowledge is no longer satisfied by a particular team, the person is free to form a new structure of connections or relationships. Each team is encouraged to link up with other teams when it appears helpful to the Body. The network is free to pursue, learn from, and act on all forms of new information on behalf of the Body. These networks involve everyone's thinking and input without slowing down the decision-making process. People solicit one another's advice without having to give them veto power.

111

The Future Is with Us

During the last fifty years a kaleidoscope of revolutionary alliances and networks has developed. The never-before-in-history, multiple-nation coalition against one country (Iraq) for its invasion of another (Kuwait) is one of the most remarkable examples. The GATT and the Free Trade Act are two more.[17]

> **Alliances and networks are at the heart of the future.**

Over the next twenty-five years churches and denominations will form alliances and networks across denominational lines. These alliances and networks will emerge for a variety of reasons: to avoid the stranglehold of bureaucracies; to carry out common ministries; and to do together what they could not do on their own.

Already, strategic new alliances are springing up, pointing the way to the twenty-first century models of ministry beyond denominational lines. Some of the most notable are Leadership Network in Tyler, Texas; Willow Creek Association in South Barrington, Illinois; and The Teaching Church Network in Burnsville, Minnesota.[18]

New alliances and networks of teams will also emerge in permission-giving churches. The self-organized team approach will be vastly different from the committee structures that are entrenched in bureaucracies.

CHAPTER 9

SELF-ORGANIZING MINISTRY TEAMS

"Perhaps the biggest reason for the movement toward empowered work teams is the fact that teams work."

Richard S. Wellins

Permission-giving churches have as few standing committees as possible (a standing committee meets on a regular schedule). The clearer a church is about its mission and the more intent it is on being a permission-giving church, the fewer standing committees it needs.

Few churches need more than one standing committee. Most churches can reach this goal over a five- or six-year period of transition. (This one committee is discussed in chapter 10.)

In the place of standing committees permission-giving churches encourage the formation of self-organizing, self-governing, and self-destructing teams. These teams can start on their

Bureaucratic Weaknesses

♦ *Self-Organizing*
♦ *Self-Governing*
♦ *Self-Destructing*

own, decide what ministry to do and how to do it, and disband when they complete their ministry. Permission-giving churches help people find a ministry to others instead of helping people find a committee on which to serve the institution.

The average pastor spends over ten hours a week going to meetings. The average congregation spends ninety people-hours considering whether or not to start a new ministry only to finally say no to most of them.[1] No matter how eager and committed leadership may be, the more standing committees a church has, the less likely the people are to have the time and energy to equip the laity and deliver ministry to and beyond the congregation. **moo**

Self-organizing teams fulfill the functions not covered by the standing committees. They are established when needed and disbanded when their task is over. The person in charge of or wanting to begin the ministry finds a team of people who want to work on that specific project and together develops the specific ministry.[2]

For example, instead of a Mission Committee, self-organizing teams exist for each of the various missions the church is engaged in. Additional teams are established when a new team wants to start a new mission. These various teams never meet with one another to decide what missions they are going to be involved in or to hear reports from the other missions, or coordinate their efforts. From time to time they collaborate with other teams to see what help they can be to each other in the pursuit of their particular missions.

Self-organizing Teams

Permission-giving churches are made up of loosely knit teams.[3] These teams are made up of autonomous

114

individuals who choose to form alliances and networks with others, often in groups, but are not bound by any loyalty to those groups.

A Ministry Team is not another form of a committee.

They are bound together primarily by the common mission of that particular church. The people on these teams have affinity for one another even though each person may bring a different spiritual gift or talent to the group.

I experienced many good examples at Colonial Hills of self-organizing teams and how they encouraged a diversified ministry. In 1982, Lyle Schaller spent two days at Colonial Hills analyzing our ministry. Here is his comment: *"Perhaps the most unusual characteristic of Colonial Hills is that it stands out as a remarkable exception to the homogeneous principle of church growth."*[4]

My first experience with ministry teams occurred in the early 1970s. A ministry team coalesced during a weekend planning retreat. One person had a dream of bringing a Vietnamese family to our city. During the weekend, she cast her vision and several people joined her in the quest. Over the next ten years, more than a hundred refugees from several countries were resettled in the U.S.

In the last seven years of consulting, I have seen this self-organizing team model emerge many times. Frazer Memorial United Methodist in Montgomery, Alabama, Bear Valley Baptist in Denver, Colorado, and First United Methodist in Tulsa, Oklahoma, are three excellent examples. Jessica Moffatt, executive pastor of First United Methodist in Tulsa, told me that "members can call me today with a new idea for ministry and be in ministry tonight." When I asked her what they do when something unacceptable happens, she responded, "It

115

hasn't happened yet. When it does, we'll take care of it."[5] Many of the emerging small group models in cell churches are self-organizing Ministry Teams.[6]

Ministry Teams may begin anytime, anyplace without having to go through a labyrinth of committees to get approval. These teams are given authority and responsibility to coordinate and control their own ministry. They decide who, when, and how to carry out the ministry. They are encouraged to network with other teams or small groups to search for information or help.

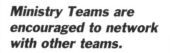

Ministry Teams are encouraged to network with other teams.

The interconnectedness of the teams is what makes the overall ministry of the church function smoothly. This network levels the organizational playing field. Each team is equal to the others and free to act without interference. The only time the governing body intervenes in the ministry of a team is if what it is doing goes against the core values of the congregation or endangers it financially.

Teams are different from committees. Committees usually come into existence because a nominating committee randomly selects people to serve together without any verification that those people want to serve, have the necessary abilities for the task, or have anything in common. Once established, committees have very little authority to make decisions. Most decisions are referred to a central committee.

Ministry Teams have affinity.

Teams, on the other hand, have affinity because each person on the team has an interest in the ministry of that particular team. They do not have to meet to decide what to do. This is decided by the team leader before he or she goes out looking for the rest of the team. The team is then responsible for making decisions and acting on its own without having to return to the source of its selection for approval.

This means that decisions are delegated to the person closest to the ministry. The organizational design is such that the space between the ministry and the people serving and being served is the smallest possible.

These teams function as "intraprises."[7] An intraprise is an autonomous enterprise within an organization. An "intrapreneur" is someone who fulfills the role of an entrepreneur within a larger organization. These teams actually form without any central supervision. A group of people see a need in the church and gather together to address and act upon the need. These teams have full authority to act on behalf of the good of the Body. These types of teams are referred to in this chapter as Ministry Teams.

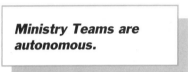

Ministry Teams are autonomous.

A system of free "intraprise" is far more democratic than a system of bureaucratic control or representative democracy. The greatest power individuals have in an open, democratic organization is not their vote for their representatives but their power to make free choices as individuals and small teams. The freedom to choose and to act on behalf of the Body is essential in the organization of the twenty-first century.

Types of Teams

Five different types of self-organizing teams have emerged over the past ten years.[8]

Problem-Solving Teams consist of knowledgeable workers who gather to solve a specific problem and then disband. I first experienced this type of team in 1986, when our church faced a serious problem. The team of about a dozen people came together out of a common interest in the health of the church. Soon they were given total freedom to solve the problem over an eighteen-month period. And they did.

Natural Management Teams consist mainly of managers of various functions within an organization. In a church, this team is usually the paid staff that guides work throughout the church. Churches with worship attendance below 500 seldom experience this form of team. This team is often the most debilitating type of team to the life of the laity because it usually tries to do ministry on behalf of the laity instead of equipping laity to do ministry.

Quality Circles, the third type of team, consist of staff and laity, and perhaps a denominational leader, who meet intermittently to air workplace problems. This form of team is in danger of extinction everywhere except in the church, where it is becoming the most popular form of team due to the rising rate of conflict.[9]

Virtual Teams are the fourth type of team. These teams are composed of people who talk to each other by computer, flying in and out as needed. This form of team will continue to grow in importance over the next two decades. For churches trying to reach people born after 1983, Virtual Teams will become one of the primary forms of lay ministry.

Work Teams are the fifth as well as the most popular type of team in both business and the church. These come and go depending on what needs to be done. Some call them a Task Force. The name Ministry Team is more consistent with the times. Ministry Teams are the self-organizing and self-managed teams that do the daily ministry of the church, such as education, worship, and missions. Used correctly, they raise the quality and diversity of ministry, cut in half the time required to begin a new ministry, raise morale among the staff and lay leadership, and spur innovation.

Ministry Teams Require

♦ **Trust**
♦ **Team Players**
♦ **Collaboration**
♦ **Restructuring**
♦ **Strong Corporate Culture**

Self-Organizing Ministry Teams

Permission-giving churches encourage every member, not just a select few, to live out their spiritual gifts by either joining or starting a small group or Ministry Team. Because small group ministries were discussed in *Dancing With Dinosaurs*, this section focuses only on Ministry Teams.[10]

Ministry Teams are self-organizing intraprises within the Body of Christ.[11] They are formed around several assumptions. (1) People closest to the ministry know what is best for that ministry. (2) Most laity want to "own" their ministry and be free to contribute to its effectiveness. (3) Teamwork develops people better than individual roles or offices.

Ministry Teams are free to form at will as long as they (1) do not violate the core values of the Body; (2) find a large enough group of people to carry out the ministry; (3) find the funds to pay for the ministry. As long as the Ministry Teams are free to self-organize, self-manage, and self-destruct, the church continues to learn and the people continue to grow. Order and coordina-

119

tion come from the networking between the various Ministry Teams and their loose connection with a staff person.

Ministry Teams plug into the network in a variety of ways. They offer help and ask for new ideas from other Ministry Teams. They go out of their way to be receptive to new ways to accomplish old ministries. They take seriously the needs, motivations, and skills of other team members when offering or receiving help or advice. They work with other team members to solve problems or carry out ministry. They rejoice in the success of another team because, like human cells, they know the success of one team is the success of another.

Ministry Teams work best if they are not added on to an already overburdened organizational structure. Most standing committees need to be eliminated. Otherwise, the church puts most of its best leadership on standing committees, leaving those leaders little time to function on Ministry Teams. Streamlining the organization is discussed in chapter 10.

If money is needed and the church cannot provide it, the group is free to raise the money in or out of the church. Some of the core Ministry Teams should be included in the budget. Core Ministry Teams are discussed below.

At this point, those familiar with bureaucracy are probably wondering how one gets control of all of this. You don't. Permission-giving

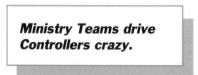

Ministry Teams drive Controllers crazy.

leaders trust people and God's spirit. Of course, some unacceptable things will happen. But many wonderful and new ministries will emerge. Don't be so concerned about making sure nothing unacceptable happens that your actions ensure that nothing new and innovative happens.

My experience as a consultant has taught me that Ministry Teams are effective when the following eight characteristics are present.

Ministry Teams have affinity either for each other or the ministry. Because of affinity, the clashing of personalities is usually absent, turf issues are less likely to be experienced, and reciprocity more likely to be present.

Ministry Team members are competent in what they want to accomplish. This competency comes not from intellect or skill but from each person's spiritual gift. They choose to work on this ministry. This gives the members faith in each other's commitment to the group process. The team is the right team for the right ministry. The members of the team excel in what they do because they enjoy it and have the spiritual gifts that match the ministry.

Ministry Teams understand and support the church's corporate culture (discussed in chapter 10). They understand how they fit into the overall mission of the church. Therefore, they are free to make on-the-spot decisions without having to get permission from a central committee or person.

Ministry Team meetings are a top priority on each person's calendar. Priority is seldom a problem because the team formed around a common interest or affinity. Therefore, the rest of the Body can count on them doing what they said they would do.

Ministry teams have a single issue to work on, which gives them a built-in agenda even before they meet.

> *Do all the meetings you attend have an agenda?*

In the case of a Core Ministry Team, the Mission State-ment of the Ministry Team is supplied by the Steering Team (described in chapter 10). In the case of many of the spontaneously formed Ministry Teams, the Mission Statement for the Ministry Team is designed by the team leader prior to the first meeting. They never meet just to meet. Most committees have to meet first to find out why they are meeting. Frustration mounts as people spend endless hours trying to find out why they are together in the first place. The key is to have a goal in place before forming a team.

Ministry Teams are not launched in a vacuum with little or no training or support. The teams are guided by the Mission and Value Statements. Also, every team has a staff liaison who supplies training or support as needed. Otherwise, the teams stay in touch with staff over the phone.

Ministry Teams require team players. Forming teams around affinity encourages a team spirit. How-ever, some people are lone wolves or creative types that never work well on teams or committees. It is unfair to ask them to work on teams. Let them work alone and hold them accountable to the culture of the congrega-tion.

Ministry Teams are autonomous as long as they stay within the boundaries of the Mission, Vision, and Value Statements. Ministry Teams are free to raise their own money within or outside of the congregation. They are free to keep whatever money they raise and use it as they see fit.

The Ministry Team Network

A network of self-generating, self-governing, self-destructing Ministry Teams can deliver a unique and customized ministry on or off church property, in a timely and consistent manner to a target audience any place, anytime, by anyone in the organization.

Ministry Teams honor the diversity of the Body.

The network of teams allows each member of the congregation to live out his or her spiritual gifts instead of doing what the institutional church wants accomplished. Uniqueness is essential in permission-giving churches. Traditional churches are too homogenized. moo Everyone acts and looks too much alike. It is not supposed to be that way in the Body of Christ. Each person is a unique gift from God with a unique ministry to share with the world. Helping each person find that gift and live out that gift is the role of organization.

Two tools of the Quantum Age make the delivery of unique, customized services more manageable. Desktop computers and people-based software are the first tool.

Permission-giving churches see computers as a major ministry tool. They purchase software on the basis of how they want to manage the value of their human resources. Computers allow churches of any size to customize their

Put money in the bank. It won't go anywhere and will gain interest. Put people in the database because they will go somewhere.

response to thousands of people in a far more effective and efficient manner than small churches, with the best intentions, have done in the past. Few investments are as important for a church as the purchase of good people-based management software. Such software allows the church to keep track of each person's spiritual gifts, the ebb and flow of Ministry Teams, small groups, and individual projects.[12]

Computers help us manage the "value" of people. People don't need to be managed. They need to be grown. People grow as they add value to themselves and to the future health and vitality of the Body of Christ. The permission-giving church determines value on the basis of personal growth. Is this member growing in her or his understanding of faith? Is this staff person a more committed and motivated person in Christ today than yesterday? Is the staff learning from its mistakes? Is the leadership able to see failure as the prelude to future breakthroughs in ministry? In my tradition we call this "going on to perfection."[13]

Most established churches do not see the human value in computers. They still see them as a tool to help the church conduct business. They choose software to help manage their financial needs. The first information they put in the computer are the financial records.

Most organizations are accustomed to managing and allocating tangible resources such as brick and mortar or programs. In permission-giving churches these tangible things will not be viewed as the most valuable or costly resources of the church. Today, it is more important to manage and allocate the intangibles such as relationships, and all forms of information, especially electronic data, time, software, and lifestyles. These are the things that bring value to an organization today. Computers will help us manage and make use of their intangible value.

The other tool that helps congregations deliver unique ministries in a timely fashion is the availability of demographic and psychographic data.[14] This data makes it possible for churches to (1) know more about the community in which we live than ever before; (2) have the capability to target whomever they wish; and (3) customize their materials and ministries to meet the physical or spiritual needs of the community because of this data.[15]

Ministry Teams allow this unique and customized service to be delivered in a timely manner. Time is the new form of money in the Quantum Age. People born after 1950 place a high premium on time and spontaneity. Time is an asset, not a limitation. The faster an organization can deliver its product the

> *The motto of permission-giving churches is any time, any place, for any one, no matter what.*

healthier that organization will be. A timely response is essential. When people are hurting, they cannot wait for the church to respond when it wants. When they want to know more about faith, they cannot wait for us to get around to them. When they need someone to listen to them, they do not have time to wait until we are free. **mOO**

The shorter the time lag between discovering a spiritual need and the implementation of a response in the form of a new ministry, the more effective the church will be in the twenty-first century. This is true for needs within the Body of Christ as well as those in the outside community.

How long is too long? It will vary from church to church depending on the spiritual depth of the people. However, some guidelines are possible. For example, a church does not need to take six months to determine the need for another worship service. It shouldn't take more than ten minutes to determine whether or not to

125

purchase a fax machine, and not ever at a board meeting. An official board should never spend time determining the new color of the toilet seat.

Core Ministry Teams

It is imperative that congregations are clear on their Core Ministry Teams. Core teams are named when the leadership cannot conceive of the church without them. Worship and Sunday School are core ministries in most churches. Therefore, the Ministry Teams connected with worship are Core Ministry Teams. At Colonial Hills, the weekday child care system was a core ministry. Whatever it took, the staff and key lay leaders did it to ensure its future. To determine the core ministries at your church ask this question: "What is it about our experience of Jesus Christ that this community cannot live without?"[16]

Core Ministry Teams do not come and go very often. They are the "staple" ministries the church cannot thrive without. They are essential to the Mission, Vision, and Values of the congregation. Each core ministry team is assigned a staff liaison.

> **Core Ministry Teams are ministries without which the church can't be healthy.**

Each team has a leader. The team leaders recruit the rest of the team. Thus, each team has an internal (lay) and external (staff) team leader. These teams receive the most attention and the most money if necessary.

One of the most important decisions churches under two hundred in worship make is deciding on their core ministries. To grow beyond two hundred, most churches have to have at least two core ministries in addition to worship and Sunday school. As the church ministers to more people, it must support and nurture more core ministries.

How to Begin Ministry Teams

First, complete the Readiness Chart in appendix 3 to determine whether or not you should even begin Ministry Teams. If you score under sixty, begin establishing teams. If not, go to chapter 10 and develop or redevelop your Mission, Vision, and Value Statements.

All staff and key leaders must give up the trappings of formal power. The team concept demands a massive change for key lay leaders. They must move from the position of "the team serves us" to "we serve the team." **moO** Finance and trustee people are a good example. In traditional churches these organizations are designed to control expenses. In traditional churches these committees control more than they liberate. Instead of understanding their responsibility to be controlling expenses or taking care of property, they need to ask the teams how they can assist them in carrying out their ministries.

Once you determine how much control your leadership is willing to give away, start there and begin to apply the Two-Year-Old Rule. Children two years old are always asking their parents for something. When they are told no, they retreat for a moment or two

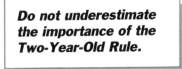

Do not underestimate the importance of the Two-Year-Old Rule.

only to return asking for the same thing. Each time they ask if they can have something, most parents are subconsciously moved closer to saying yes, to their request.

So start where your leaders are and gently push them into giving more and more permission.

Ensure that all teams fit into the value statement. Work at erring on the side of permission giving.

> **High levels of learning from Team work.**

Allow teams to develop at their own pace. Moving from a closed system to an open system is an evolutionary process or journey. Some teams crawl, walk, run, drive, or fly from one destination to another. So work with them where they are. Each team will be different. Some can start off making every decision including budgeting. Others will need to have some hand holding along the way. Both are okay and immanently better than a controlled system.

Teams grow more responsible as they assume more ownership. Teams will assume ownership as more individuals function autonomously in a team atmosphere, in a variety of settings, over a period of time. However, how fast teams can develop depends more on how quickly the old-line leaders can adjust than how ready the team leaders are. The more freedom given, the more responsibility assumed. The more responsibility assumed, the more growth. The more growth, the better the quality that begins to emerge.

Provide extensive training for the teams and team leadership. Sharing leadership and working in teams does not come naturally for many people, especially those born before World War Two. The type and nature of training varies from team to team depending on the complexity of the ministry

> **Resource, Resource, Resource.**

and the maturity of the individuals who make up the team. It is best if the external team leader provides the necessary coaching before the team takes action, not after. The external team leader should not be a problem solver because people grow best when they solve their own problems. Coaches ask what the team needs to deal with its issues and solve its problems.

Key questions that must be asked as churches make the transition to Ministry Teams.

- Who can withhold permission from new ministries? How?
- How will teams be structured?
- What will the boundaries be?
- Which are the Core Ministry Teams?
- How will each team handle the need for money?
- How will we measure the outcome of the teams' efforts in relationship to the Body?
- How can the facilities be arranged to support the teams?
- How will teams get the information they need to manage their own ministries?
- What training will the church need to make the transition into team ministry?
- How will we publicly recognize effective teams in order to encourage more of the same quality?
- How will the teams assess their own performance?
- What systems must be modified to support the teams?
- What obstacles might be encountered along the way from long-time members with vested interests?
- How long are we going to give this process before we pass judgment on its success?
- How fast are we going to make the transition to total decision making by the teams?

If you decide to begin a team ministry, avoid the following mistakes. (1) Don't use someone else's organization. Develop your own so that all teams support the mission of the church. (2) Don't abdicate responsibility. Even though teams are given total decision-making power, it is essential that an accountability system is provided. (3) Don't refuse help from someone outside of the church if you have never ministered in a permission-giving church. (4) Don't abandon the project before its time. Give it three to five years. (5) Don't make the transition to team ministry without beginning to dismantle some of the bureaucracy.

CHAPTER 10

THE STEERING TEAM

"The greatest power individuals have in democratic organizations is not their vote for representatives. Nor is it the influence their ideas have in conferences. The greatest power is in making free choices as individuals and as small teams."
Gifford & Elizabeth Pinchot

The purpose of organization in permission-giving churches is to provide the environment in which individuals live out their spiritual gifts in the everyday world and pass on to others what they are learning about the application of their spiritual gifts to daily living. If a church emphasizes spiritual gifts, it is essential that it also gives permission for everyone to use his or her spiritual gifts. This organization is worlds apart from a committee-driven congregation and representative democracy.

Most congregations are governed by some form of representative democracy. A congregation gives authority to a

> **Not only is it disastrous for leaders to encourage people to discover what God created them to do and then tell them they can't use their gifts, it is also unethical.**

select group of members to oversee its affairs and direct its ministry. This select group is supposed to represent the interests of the congregation. However, it usually works that the leadership makes sure the organization "runs" as efficiently as possible by balancing the budget, keeping good minutes, following parliamentary procedure, faithful attendance, and so on. All of which can make everyone look busy while nothing is accomplished other than "running the organization."   moo

Representative democracy is harmful to the Body of Christ because it ensures that only a few people blossom and apply their spiritual gifts. A few people, the permission-givers, control what most people can do and too many people are involved in decision making. Usually, these people either have money, desire power, or have been members the longest.

In most congregations the governing body assumes too wide a range of responsibility and authority for the Body of Christ to be effective. Whatever organizational system prevails, anyone wishing to begin a new ministry has to go through several layers of organization in order to ask the governing body for permission before they act in the service of the Lord.

In an effort to make the governing body truly representative, many congregations put too many people on the governing body. About all the body can do is vote "yes," "no," or

> *In the quantum world churches will be more effective with just one standing committee.*

"let's think about this some more." Members often leave meetings either feeling that all they do is rubber-stamp something as if there were not enough time for discussion, or as if nothing is ever accomplished.[1]

The goal of the governing body in permission-giving congregations is to serve a much different function. Permission-giving congregations function best if they are held accountable by one small standing committee. I call this group the Steering Team.[2] This group consists of no more than seven people, including the pastor. The group is limited to a two year term to ensure that if they become a cork instead of a funnel, they can't obstruct ministry very long.

The Steering Team takes the place of all committees. Any committee, in one way or another, is an obstacle to permission giving. Finance and Trustee people often determine more of the program of the church than the people in charge of the programs because so much programming in a church depends on either getting funding or permission for one or both of these committees. These committees seldom think about how their decisions affect the lives and growth of people. Usually, all they are concerned with is making financial ends meet or keeping the facilities clean and neat.

The Steering Team (perhaps like the deacons of the early church) are role models and servants instead of nominated members. These people need to be visibly practicing servants of Jesus Christ and one another. Permission giving is not an attempt to foster the claims of the individual rights movement of the 1980s and 1990s. Just as patriotic citizenship was the framework for the definition of civic freedom within a democratic society, so freedom to exercise one's spiritual gift is the framework of the definition of the Body of Christ. Do not confuse freedom to use our spiritual gifts with individual rights. We are free from our sin, but we are not free to do as we please. We give up all rights when we decide to follow Christ. We are servants of Christ and one another. Exercising our spiritual gifts on behalf of the Body of Christ is the way we serve.

The role of the Steering Team is to be the central nervous system of the Body. It encourages the strategies, policies, values, beliefs, and principles of the congregation; ensures coordination between the staff, lay leaders, and various Ministry Teams; meets monthly to ensure that the ministry of the church is progressing according to the congregational plan; and provides an accountability system when necessary.

The Steering Team provides an environment in which people are free to exercise their spiritual gifts without having to ask for permission. People need to have a safe and friendly place in which to develop the gifts God has given them. The Steering Team encourages and supports each individual in exercising his or her

> *People closest to the point of ministry know best how to do that ministry.*

gift, developing new teams, and establishing new ministries by making as few decisions as possible. The Steering Team also goes to great lengths to err on the side of giving permission for new ministries to emerge by saying yes to as many new ideas and ministries as possible; it also allows on-the-spot decision making by the people closest to the issue.

The Steering Team provides an environment in which freedom, diversity, and choices are the operational words. When times get tough, bureaucratic organizations tend to introduce more choice into the organization. People in crises seek help everywhere. Relationships and roles cross all sorts of boundaries. Unfortunately, when the storm is over, bureaucratic organizations return to the more cumbersome structure they had been using.

134

The Steering Team provides the environment in which defined boundaries guide people as they choose how to live out their spiri-

> **Boundaries of opportunity replace spans of control.**

tual gift for the sake of the Body. Every church, no matter how fluid, must have some form of boundaries. Defined boundaries help churches avoid having meetings to approve or disapprove of new ideas and ministries; ensure corporate order in the midst of individual and team freedom; and reduce the presence of fear during transition.

Contrary to bureaucracy, which spells out what is to be done and who has what powers, permission-giving organizations define the boundaries in which ministry can occur, leaving the networks of individuals and teams free to exercise their spiritual gifts. These boundaries are seen as the *opportunities* in which every member of the congregation can engage in ministry, instead of as rules, regulations, or limitations.

Through some form of congregational process, a church must first develop a corporate culture. In his book *Creating Corporate Culture,* Charles Hampden-Turner says, "Corporate culture comes from within people and is put together by them to reward the capacities that they have in common."[3] Corporate culture consists of the values and beliefs that define the congregation. It is the context in which on-the-spot decisions are made and learning takes place; the basis for rewarding good decisions; the synergy that holds the permission-giving network together and allows for autonomous action on the part of individuals and teams; the basis for accountability; the identity of the Body in the midst of rapid change; and the environment that brings out the best of each person. For our purposes, I refer to corporate church culture as Body culture.

Three documents form the Body culture of permission-giving congregations. They are the Mission Statement, Vision Statement, and the Value Statement.[4] These three statements give a clear, distinct,

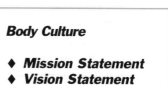

Body Culture

♦ **Mission Statement**
♦ **Vision Statement**
♦ **Value Statement**

and focused picture of what God is calling the church to be and do.[5]

The Mission Statement is the basic, bottom-line mission of the church. It is why the church exists. It is what keeps the leaders and various teams in alignment. The more diverse the ministries of the church are, the more important the Mission Statement is.[6] It is seldom longer than a sentence, is easily memorized, and general in nature.

The Vision Statement is the narrow mission of the church. It is slightly longer and much more specific. It steers individuals and teams in the direction a particular Body is going and tells them what the Body hopes to accomplish. A church must be clear about its bottom line in order to develop Mission and Vision Statements.[7]

The Value Statement sets the *boundaries of opportunity* in which individuals and groups within the congregation can live out the above two statements without having to get permission to act. It provides the subtle boundaries that informally sanction or prohibit behavior.

Consider the following examples of these three statements.

Mission Statement:

To honor our Lord and Savior, Jesus Christ, by carrying out his command to make disciples of all nations.

Vision Statement:

We believe God has called us to reach the unchurched in the surrounding areas and to challenge the existing social structures. We further intend to multiply our ministry by planting churches, by preparing our people for leadership roles in vocational ministry and para-church groups, by sending out missionaries, becoming a teaching center for people of all denominations, and forming alliances and networks with like-minded groups regardless of denominational affiliation.

Value Statement:

A commitment to relevant, biblical preaching: We are committed to equipping Christians, through the preaching and teaching of God's Word, to follow Christ in every sphere of life.

A commitment to the Body of Christ: We are committed to collaborative networks of autonomous people and groups using their spiritual gifts for the common good of the Body of Christ.

A commitment to prayer: The ministries and activities of this church will be characterized by a reliance on prayer in their conception, planning, and execution.

A commitment to lay ministry: Whenever possible, the ministries of this church will be carried out by nonordained servants. This will be accomplished through training opportunities and through practices that encourage lay initiative, leadership, responsibility, and authority in various ministries of the church.

A commitment to the value of every person: We are committed to all people just as they are without regard for race, faith, culture, lifestyle, or whatever. We value the dialogue and friendship between people of differing perspectives.

A commitment to small groups: We are committed to small-group ministry because it is where most individual transformation, conversion, and leadership development takes place.

A commitment to the Holy Spirit: We are committed to spiritual creativity and innovation. We are open to continual evaluation of our mission because we are more concerned with effectiveness in ministry than with adherence to tradition or efficiency.

A commitment to excellence: We seek to maintain a high standard of excellence in all of our ministries. This will be achieved when every person is exercising his or her God-given spiritual gift to the best of his or her ability.

A commitment to growth: We believe that life is meant to be given away and that Christianity exists to share Christ with others. Therefore, we will pursue attitudes and knowledge that unobtrusively encourage numerical growth without compromising in any way our integrity or our commitment to biblical truth.

These three statements give direction about what can and cannot be done with the property or who can or cannot use the property. Once they are in place and recognized by the congregation, the Steering Team encourages individuals and teams to freely choose how and when to live out their spiritual gifts and begin new ministries. People are permitted to make on-the-spot decisions, even they cost money.[8]

The Steering Team provides an environment in which support is freely given to the core (essential) ministries of the church. Core ministries differ from church to church, but they all have one thing in common—they are essential to the heart and soul of that particular church. Most of the money in an organization should go to help accomplish these core ministries.

The Steering Team provides an environment that ensures organizational standards for accounting, and financial support of staff. This can be accomplished by one of the seven members on the Steering Team having an accounting degree or, better still, by arranging for a yearly or quarterly audit by an independent CPA. If a Finance Committee is absolutely necessary,

Trustees and Finance people should see themselves as the servants of those doing ministry with people.

then ensure that its primary role is to provide as much money for ministry as possible and to discover and implement ways to help more people discover the joy of being stewards of all they have and own, and not simply raising money and balancing budgets. If you absolutely must have **moo** Trustees that are separate from any other position or committee, then ensure that their role is more to provide places where people can be equipped and ministries can occur than to merely take care of buildings. **moo**

The Steering Team provides an environment in which order exists and accountability is ensured. There are times when things go so

The Steering Team holds people accountable instead of trying to control them.

139

astray, or someone takes advantage of their freedom or breaks the boundaries of the Value Statement, that the person has to be held responsible for his or her actions. Any person or team that does not work for the Body must be held accountable in ways that are in line with the values of the congregation. Otherwise, the Statements have no meaning.

Organizational structure must be simple and fluid in order to facilitate the mission. Structures set in concrete are not effective today. Most older church members, however, see strategies or plans as set in concrete. To talk about changing what they have worked many years to develop is threatening. So proceed with caution and expect resistance.

CHAPTER 11

TRANSFORMATION

"Taking the Quantum Leap means taking a risk, going off into an uncharted territory with no guide to follow."

Fred Alan Wolf

"Yet surely this is a time to **make the future**—precisely because everything is in flux. This is a time for action."

Peter Drucker

The vast majority of established churches are "stuck" in some form of control, resulting in a plateau or decline.   m00   Stuck churches have numerous rules, policies, and regulations; are top down, permission-withholding structures; encourage lots of paper trails and red tape; experience passivity by most and rulership by a few; emphasize precedence and procedure; emphasize efficiency and saving money; are concerned more about counting money than reaching people; reward fine-tuners and avoid innovators; do not give committees the power to act; and always read the minutes of the last meeting.

This chapter is de-voted to "unsticking" or transforming plateaued or declining congregations into permission-giving congregations. A nine-step process is offered. This process has been used the last seven years in a variety of denominations in the U.S. and Canada. When followed, the success rate is better than 75 percent.[1]

Many books have been written on the process of transforming an organization. Most of them make far too much of the logistics involved. The process is simple; the sacrifice is often great. Transformation takes focus, tenacity, and a willingness to be crucified! Transformation is successful when God's people understand the high stakes for which they are playing. The problem with too many of our church leaders is that they no longer see ministry as a life-and-death issue. Too many clergy are professionals; too many laity see the church as just another association or club.

Nine Step Process

♦ **Pastor's Commitment**
♦ **Congregational Context**
♦ **Understanding the Community**
♦ **Committed Leadership**
♦ **Casting a Vision**
♦ **Developing a Team Ministry**
♦ **Developing a Plan**
♦ **Implementation**
♦ **Institutionalization**

Step One: The pastor's commitment

The process of transformation almost always begins with a pastor. The pastor must be a role model for the transformation process and the laity must implement the transformation. I have reviewed dozens of case studies from both the business and the religious world, and they all say the same thing: "stuck" organizations do not become "unstuck" without a leader who (1) intentionally or unintentionally decides it is time the congregation got "unstuck"; (2) shares a new vision so articulately that it becomes a shared vision; (3) gets enough people to share

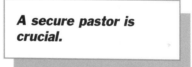

A secure pastor is crucial.

the vision to unstick the organization. Often, a fourth action accompanies transformation. The pastor leads the congregation in a rather quick and decisive victory that develops a "can do" attitude that begins to reshape the Body culture.

Pastors must be self-differentiated from the congregational system. This means that pastors intentionally act differently from the congregation. They need to know the desires of the congregation, but that does not mean that self-differentiated pastors have the same desires. What congregations want may not be what they need. The ability of a pastor to discern the subjective difference between actual and implied needs is often wanting, but self-differentiated pastors must be willing to make these refinements if they want to transform a church.

Pastor and spouse must decide what they are NOT willing to risk before they begin tinkering with the life of a congregation. Self-differentiation threatens the status quo and upsets the homeostasis of the system, which inevitably leads to conflict. Therefore, the pastor needs to know what his or her family is willing to risk to bring about transformation.

Make a list of what you are NOT willing to risk. The more items you have on your list, the less likely it is that you will be able to transform a congregation. Most pastors I talk with who are growing or transforming churches tell me that the only thing they have on their list is their family. They also tell me that the process of growth or transformation is the number one threat to their family life. Four out of five pastors with whom I work tell me that pastoral ministry is affecting their family life negatively. Given the apostle Paul's admonitions, this should be no surprise to those who are called to choose a transforming ministry.

143

Pastors and their spouses will probably face one or more of the following stress points when attempting to transform a congregation.[2] (1) Controllers are pressured to leave office; (2) the traditional emphasis on "running the church or organization" is abandoned; (3) nominations are replaced by spiritual gifting; (4) new leadership makes mistakes trying to implement innovation; (5) money in the bank is spent instead of saved for a rainy day; (6) high commitment is a prerequisite to joining and leadership; (7) Trustees, Finance, and Music Directors are no longer the focus of power or decision making; (8) laity are expected to do quality ministry; (9) traditional organizational structures are streamlined; (10) contemporary worship is developed; (11) church leaders are in need of retooling to continue the transformation; (12) large numbers of new members begin to attend, join, and seek to do ministry; (13) new ministries outnumber and sometimes replace traditional ministry; (14) ministry is designed as much for young adults as for older, long-term members; (15) staff must be replaced because they are not team players.

Pastors must decide if they are the type of person who can lead a congregation through transformation. Some questions to ask are: How much income do I need to live? What size church can I pastor the best? What is my best gift that I bring to the ministry? What do I deeply believe God wants me to do with my life? What standards will I use to gauge the outcome of my ministry? What do I primarily want to

> *It is one thing to want to transform a congregation; it is another to have the gifts and graces.*

144

accomplish during my life? What do I want to be doing two, five, ten, and twenty years from now?

Several inventories are available to help pastors decide if they are the type to transform a congregation. The Myers-Briggs Type Indicator suggests that NTs and NFs are the best suited for transformation and SJs are the least suited. Js or Ps can be change agents but they have to constantly work on those areas that will get in the way of them pressing for transition. Ps have to work on being more decisive and Js have to be careful not to become too rigid and inflexible. Fs need to work on not giving up the vision over the long haul.[3]

The Birkman Method is one of the finest tools I have seen to date to help individuals pinpoint their unique personality traits and make maximum use of these God-given gifts in all dimensions of life. The method reveals the areas most likely to cause stress by helping a pastor look within himself or herself for the church environment that is ideally suited to his or her spiritual gifts. This same instrument, when instituted within the laity, aids in volunteer placement and small-group facilitation; within the staff, it is an excellent team-building tool.[4]

Visualize the church twenty years from now as you would like to see it and begin to formulate God's vision. What does it look like? What will it take to make this vision become reality? Once you are clear about the vision and can articulate it, share it at every possible opportunity. The following questions are helpful in formulating a vision.

> Will our church focus ministry primarily on the needs within our congregation or will we focus as much attention on the needs of the unchurched in the community as we do on ourselves?

Can a church be a church without concerning itself about the unchurched around it?

Are we going to be a church that depends mostly on the pastor for congregational care and evangelistic outreach or are we going to develop a lay-driven ministry that incorporates both pastoral care and evangelistic outreach?

Are we going to be a program-based church that invites people to attend programs led by professional staff, or are we going to be a small group-based church that relies less on program and staff and more on the priesthood of believers and the lay networking of members and friends outside the church?

Are we going to be basically a Sunday church or are we going to be a seven-day-a-week church and, if so, what are the core ministries during the week?

Will all of our ministries be conducted on the church property, or will we develop satellite ministries?

Are we content with developing worship designed basically for people who are over fifty or who may be under fifty but have never left the church, or are we going to also provide worship designed for people especially in their twentys and thirtys who have left the church?

What does Acts say about the role of stewardship of money in our lives and are we living up to the New Testament understanding of tithing?

146

Are we willing to staff the church in order to reach the unchurched or will we remain staffed as we are?

Take the long-term view. Transformation seldom happens overnight. It usually takes three to five years, sometimes much longer. Patience is essential. It is best if you form a mental image of where you would like the church to be in twenty years. The

> **Transformation may take longer than most pastors are willing to stay.**

rate at which change can occur depends on the skill of the leader and leadership team, the context in which the change is to occur, and the discontentment level of the leadership.

However, look for a quick victory. The victory is important to rekindle confidence in the church leadership. Often "stuck" churches have not had what they would call a victory in a long time. The smaller the congregation, the stronger the need for a victory. A victory is something the church has not been able to accomplish but has wished it could. The victory does not have to be big. The more defeated a congregation is, the smaller the victory can be and the larger it will appear.

Step Two—The congregational context[5]

Call into question everything the church believes and practices. At the beginning of transformation, no one knows a Sacred Cow from that which is relevant to our time. We think we do, and that's the problem. Unless we question everything, the very things we withhold from the process are likely to be our Sacred Cows. Anything less leaves us with too many unexam-

> **Sacred Cows masquerade as our closest friends.**

ined practices and beliefs that will lead to homeostasis.[6] This organizational step is not done in public nor discussed with key leaders. It is an internal audit of one's ability to see the origins of the problems and thus the solutions. Often, this is the primary role a consultant can play.

Complete my "Ministry Audit" in the back of *The Church Growth Handbook* **or contact me for an updated copy of the audit.**[7] The "Ministry Audit" gives you everything you need to know about the congregation to begin the process of transformation. *The Church Growth Handbook* is also a handy guide for answering any of the questions you might have about the "Ministry Audit". If used annually, the "Ministry Audit" can become a benchmark to evaluate your progress, and help you spot developing trends before they become a serious problem.

Decide where the congregation is on the S curve. Charles Handy has done an invaluable service to organizations in his development of the S curve.[8] This model is far more helpful in the Quantum world than the Bell Curve that is so often used.

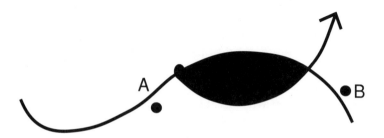

The goal is to start a new S curve before the first one ends. The right place to start the second curve is at point A while the church still has the time, energy, and resources to get the new curve through its initial stages before the first curve plateaus and declines. At point A all the messages received by the organization indicate that everything is fine.

> **If it ain't broke, fix it.**

The second curve is going to be different from the first. Those who lead the second curve are often not the people who led the first curve. For a time, new ideas and new people have to co-exist with the old until the second curve is established and the first begins to wane. I call this the "two-track system." The shaded area becomes a time of great confusion because two or more groups of people and sets of ideas are competing for the future. Alternative forms of worship are one of the best examples of this shaded area.

Step Three—The needs of the area surrounding the church

Most church members think they know their community when they don't. I was in a Florida community that had been known for years as a retirement area. The church offered nothing for young adults, children, or youth. The average age of those in worship was over sixty. However, I noticed on the way to the church a number of public schools. I also knew that 51 percent of the population was under fifty years of age. When I arrived, I asked them why there were no young adults in the church. They responded by saying that this is a retirement area. When they saw the demographics they were astounded. Over the next two years they added a worship service and programs designed to reach young adults. During that period of time the church grew from 300 to 450 in worship.[9]

Demographic and psychographic materials can help church leaders asses the area around a church. Several such studies exist that go beyond what can be found in the U.S. Census or any local projections.[10] Demographic and psychographic studies focus the church outward instead of inward. They tell us who is in the community, which generation or lifestyle is growing or declining, who the church should target, how hard or easy it will be to grow this church, how much income the church could have, and how the church compares to the community. Once a clear picture is formed about the community, the congregation is ready to develop ministries that target some part of it.[11]

Focus Groups augment demographic information about the community.[12] The purpose of a Focus Group is to identify the attitudes and needs of a targeted group of people. Choose the lifestyle you want to reach and invite seven to ten people who fit this description to spend an hour and a half in a group process. The facilitator asks them nonleading questions. Such questions as "What is it like to be thin. . . ?" "How would you compare your situation today with that of your parents at your present stage of life?" "Have there been any times in your life when the church has played an important role?" "What place does God play in your life?" The facilitator then listens to the responses, reads between the lines, and is not afraid to let the group fill in the silence.[13]

Step Four—The condition of the leadership

Complete the Permission-Giving Readiness Test in Appendix 3. It will give you some indication of where to begin the transformation process, how fast you can implement transformation, and how long it might take to transform the congregation.

Determine the number of Controllers. The goal is either to convert or neutralize them even if it means they leave the church. How many are in official leadership and how many play a determining role without holding any office? Where are the Controllers located? If the Controllers are less than 10 percent of the leadership, you have a green light no matter how controlling the person may be. This does not mean you won't have a miserable time breaking their control.   **mOO**   If the Controllers occupy more than 10 percent of the leadership, a real challenge is in front of you. Meet and pray with these individuals. Discover which of their friends or family are positive about a new direction for the church and encourage them to work on the Controllers. Equip the leaders in favor of transformation to become the flying wedge between you and the Controllers. Let them take the heat and you support, nurture, and encourage them. This allows the pastor to continue to be the pastor to individuals against the transformation.

Pastors must never forget that their first priority, even in the midst of being a catalyst of change, is to be the spiritual leader to those who are hurting because their world is changing.[14] The feelings people have while seeing their beloved church transformed are comparable to the grief experienced over the loss of a loved one. The bigger the need for transformation, the bigger the need for the pastor to be the pastor. This makes the flying wedge more important than ever.

Determine the willingness of the leadership to break the existing rules. A willingness on the part of leadership to change, break, and/or eliminate the rules opens the door for change. As the church moves further into the permission-giving mode, all individuals are given permission to break the rules if by doing so the values of the church are enhanced.

Rules served us well when the future was relatively predictable. It was possible to make rules that would work. During times of quantum leaps, it is impossible to make rules that will make sense for very long because the context in which the rules were instituted no longer exists.

In the days of the one-day-a-week church, it made sense to have controls on who could or could not use the facilities. When churches were Sunday experiences consisting of primarily worship and church school, it made sense to require an adult to be present whenever children or youth wanted to use the gymnasium. It made sense for Trustees to take care of the day-to-day maintenance needs of the church because they had all week to fix whatever needed fixing. Today those rules no longer make sense because healthy churches are seven-day-a-week churches and it is impossible to have the facilities open every day, always have an adult present, and for the Trustees to fix things on a daily basis. In the same way, it no longer makes sense for Trustees to decide who can use the facilities. Today it works best if the office secretary makes those decisions on a daily basis based on her understanding of the mission of the church.

Permission-giving churches exchange rules for values. In changing times it is more important that we are clear on our common values, beliefs, and mission than to have agreed-upon rules. In the permission-giving church, the ability to change rules is decentralized so that anyone can change the rules if, by doing so, the Mission, Vision, and Value Statements are not changed or hampered.

On the other hand, some rules are necessary for people to know how to behave in a changing environment.

Churches wanting to become permission-giving churches need to develop what Benveniste calls "meta rules."[15]

Meta rules are the agreed-upon rules an organization will follow in breaking the rules. In other words, it is not

Meta rules are rules made for breaking rules.

enough to throw all the rules out the window. Transformational rules are essential. Meta rules provide continuity during times of transformation. Church leaders will find the following meta rules helpful.

1. It is okay to change, break, or eliminate some rules.

2. Our Mission, Vision, and Value Statements are more important to our future than our existing rules or policies.

3. The fewer rules and policies we have the better.

4. We will err on the side of giving permission to innovative ministries.

5. It is better to innovate, make mistakes, and ask for forgiveness than it is to safeguard the status quo.

6. As we are comfortable, we will expand the ability to make on-the-spot decisions to everyone trying to live out their spiritual gifts.

7. Providing ministry is more important than balancing the budget or paying the pastor/staff.

8. It is better for buildings to be used than for them to be clean.

9. It is better to provide ministry than to have money in the bank.

10. Ministry should be provided to meet the needs of all ages based on what each age group, inside and outside the church, says will help them grow in their faith.

11. The leadership wants as few people making decisions and as many people in ministry as possible.

12. No one can be in the same decision making position more than three years at a time.

13. We will reassign our financial and human resources into those areas that have the most potential for the future health of this congregation.

14. We will continue to nurture and support the present membership of the church but not to the exclusion of the unchurched.

15. The leadership will encourage and support bottom-up innovation.

16. We will ask everyone to give an account of what they have done instead of making everyone get permission before they act.

17. We will take seriously any innovative idea for ministry, no matter how off-the-wall it may seem at the time.

18. We will reward innovation among our staff even if the new ministry fails.

19. We will emphasize a span of care instead of a span of control.

20. We will try to make our decisions based more on how we think they will affect the church twenty years from now than on how they affect us today.

21. We are willing to take risks and to manage the errors.

22. We will organize in ways that facilitate and encourage new ministries.

Have your leaders rate how they feel about the above twenty-two questions. Use a scale of 1 to 10 with 1 being total agreement and 10 being total disagreement. The lower the score the easier it is to transform the church into a permission-giving church. A score above 44 means transformation will be harder and take longer.

Step Five—Cast your vision

People begin to see the vision more by how their leaders live than by what they say.

Be a role model of permission-giving. Most church leaders have far more freedom in making decisions, delegating decisions, and giving permission than they think they have or are willing to take. Delegate and give permission whenever possible. Mentor those who are willing. Err on the side of giving people permission to begin new ministries instead of asking for permission. When you overstep your authority, ask for forgiveness. If you have a paid staff at your church, they must also be a role model of permission-giving.

Deploy the Two-Year-Old Rule. Two- and three-year-old children spend most of their waking moments discovering how far they can push their parents. When they reach their parents' limits, they back off. As soon as they sense the time is right, they are back asking their parents for the very same thing they were denied moments earlier. Church leaders need to gently push the congregation to the edge of their limits and then back

155

off. After a brief breather, come at them again with the same issue. In her book *Danger in the Comfort Zone,* Judith Bardwick says that moving an organization out of entitlement to productivity means moving them either into anxiety or fear.[16] The key is not to push the congregation so far so fast that they become angry or paralyzed. When either happens, the ministry of the church shuts down and often the pastor loses credibility.

Go as slow as prayer will let you. Develop a strong devotional and study life. Continually seek God's guidance and don't get in front of or behind God's leadership. Instead, go along side by side with God's leadership.

Step Six—Select the leadership team

Cast your vision as often and as articulately as you can and see whose eyes light up. Spend time with those people whose eyes light up. Encourage them to mold the vision into a shared vision they can talk about with authenticity.[17] From this group, develop a leadership team. Seven, including the pastor, is the best

> **Avoid the Controllers who will try to occupy all of your time.**

number; nine is the maximum. Look for two people born after 1950, two people born before 1950, and two people who have joined the church within the last year or two. Spend as much of your time as you can focusing on the team. Nothing is as important as this time.

Later, this group needs to become larger, especially if the change is radical. If the change requires a vote, this group needs to grow by including people who vote. You should be looking for these people all along the process.

The goal is for this team to either become recognized by the church leadership as a legitimate group or for it to become an official group within the church. It is most helpful when some of the people on the leadership team are already respected leaders of the church.

Step Seven—Develop a simple plan

It is one thing to have a vision. It is another thing to be able to put that vision into action. However, keep the plan simple. Avoid analysis paralysis.

Develop a win-win plan. Psychologists tell us that motivation is highest when the probability of success is fifty-fifty. People do not get involved easily if what they are being asked to do is too hard or too painful. Avoid the word *change.*   m00   Instead, talk about adding new ministries and providing choices.

Two of the most rewarding win-win new core ministries I've found are alternate worship styles and small group cell ministries. An alternate service designed for people born after 1950, that the old guard does not have to attend, is a winning choice for those who want to see the church healthy. Small group ministries can be started without ever taking a vote. A pastor merely spends the time finding a small group of leaders who are willing to be

> **Can you find three or more people with whom you can begin sharing on a regular basis?**

equipped in small group facilitation, and the process is begun. If the process is successful and the groups multiply as they should, the rest of the church is absorbed into the system.[18] Dilution is one way to overcome the Controllers.

Establish the reasons for changing the organization. Be clear and consistent in why transformation is essential. Some of the more common and helpful reasons are: (1) the desire to be more effective in nurturing and equipping people; (2) the desire to have more lay people in actual ministry to people instead of spending time in meetings; (3) the desire to reach more people effectively; (4) the paid and unpaid staff are burning out or have reached their ministry capacity and there is still more to accomplish; (5) the church has outgrown its ability to continue to respond to those who are joining; (6) the inactive membership continues to grow; (7) time is as much a pressing issue today for a large section of adults as money; and (8) most young adults will not attend meetings but will involve themselves in hands-on ministry.

Detail the vision in writing. Consider every possible scenario or contingency. List all of the reasons the church should or should not adopt this new course of action.

The following questions are helpful in planning: What do we feel God wants our church to be? What is our mission now? What will our mission be? What should our mission be? What are the implications of this in the future? What is worth and not worth doing well? What do we do now to be ready for God's future? What are the right risks to take? What are our options if this scenario works or does not work? What do we stop doing to free up time and energy? What new things do we start doing? When do we have to start to be ready? Who is chosen to implement the action? How is our planning best implemented? What is the discontentment level?

Develop a method for managing the vision. This is the part that keeps life sane. What kind of evaluation tool is needed to standardize the quality of ministry?

What kind of conflict management will we use? What role will staff play? What kind and size of staff will work best in pursuit of this vision? How will staff be brought on board? What type of delegation skills will we employ? How will we evaluate each other? What procedure will we use to process knowledge? What kind of computer system will we ultimately need? What type of information system do we need? How will we inspire in others the ability to dream and to initiate new ideas? How will we integrate the vision with every part of the Body?

Step Eight—Implementation

This step is taken only when the leadership team has refined the ministry or vision to a point that they can articulate it in a passionate way. The goal of this step is to gain permission to begin a new pilot ministry that will be evaluated in eighteen months to two years. It is best to begin a new ministry as a pilot project because those opposed are usually more open to a two-year pilot than something they think will be around forever. Often, many in opposition will come to accept the pilot as one of their own ministries.

The leadership team shares its excitement for the pilot ministry with the governing body of the church or the entire congregation, both in writing and in person. They list the reasons they support the pilot as well as its benefits to the congregation and then say something like: "Here is our idea for a new pilot ministry we would like the church to consider trying for eighteen months. We know there are many unanswered questions and

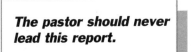

The pastor should never lead this report.

there will be a lot of difficulties along the way. We feel it has enough merit to bring it to you for your consideration. We'd like your feedback."

Never leave the impression that a decision has to be made at this time. Take notes on the comments of church members. Do not defend the pilot. Just list the benefits, the problems, and the resistance heard and sensed in their conversation.

After the meeting with the official body/board, the leadership team brainstorms about (1) how to address the problems and questions raised by the official body/board, (2) increase the benefits, and (3) disarm the resistance. Research any problem or question the official body/board had and develop strategies that minimize each concern. Make a chart of the benefits of the pilot and make sure the staff and leadership team can live with both the benefits and the hardships involved in bringing the pilot to reality.

Mail the results to the official body/board prior to the next meeting. This gives them time to review the material at home. If some respond negatively or become angry, they do so at home. People who get angry at a public meeting find it much more difficult to change their position on an issue than people who get angry in private. Sending the material to their homes prior to a meeting gives people time to become more comfortable with the new idea. If their original anger is during a church meeting it will always be more violent and negative and is harder for them to back away from in the future.

> *If I get mad at home, I have room to change my mind later. If I get mad in public, I have little room to change my mind later.*

160

Bring the official body/board back together and show them the result of the leadership team's effort. Tell them, "We have not solved all of the concerns you shared at the last meeting, but we don't think that any of these concerns are as harmful to our future as continuing to take the path the church is on at the moment. We see no better direction for our church. We are ready to pursue this vision and we hope you are ready to try it with us for eighteen months."

If it appears that the official body has too many remaining questions or concerns and

> **Remember the Two-Year-Old Rule.**

that a vote is necessary, which may not be positive, repeat the process over again including mailing them another draft of your further brainstorming.

When it appears that the official body will give the pilot ministry a favorable vote, ask the official body to join the leadership team in two weeks of prayer for God's guidance prior to the meeting in which the vote will be taken. During these two weeks recruit five positive people who are not on the leadership team to be present the night of the vote and ask

> **If you are feeling queazy at this point, remember that the Controllers are busily lining up their votes.** mOO

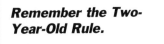

the first questions at the meeting. These questions must express a positive feeling toward the study. A positive start is essential because at most meetings there are enough people on the fence to determine the outcome of the vote. If the atmosphere is negative, they tend to vote against the new ministry. If the atmosphere is positive, they vote for the new ministry. Some call this *strategy*. Others call it *manipulation*.

The day of the meeting call all of the positive people and remind them of the meeting. Negative people seldom let anything keep them from attending the meeting; positive people are never as passionate about anything. That's why absentee voting in the past was usually against whatever was being voted on.

Expect conflict. moo Messing with sacred cows is smelly business. The Leadership Team needs to understand that anytime the attempt is made to transform a congregation, a vocal few will strongly oppose the change. moo Often pastors in churches that have started to grow, after decades of decline, will spend up to 30 percent of their time dealing with conflict. Sooner or later, this kind of attention must stop if the process of transformation is to continue.

How the leadership responds to conflict determines much of the outcome. Never overreact or take conflict personally. Pastors who take conflict personally seldom recover. Separate fact from fiction and emotion. If there is a valid issue, do not attempt to hide it or ignore it. Let the lid off of the boiling pot often enough to release the pressure. Distinguish between those individuals who are normally against issues and are dysfunctional and those who have valid concerns. Spend some time with those who have valid concerns.

In attempting to determine the depth or breadth of the conflict do not be fooled by "they." When someone says "they said" or "there are several who feel this way," you are probably speaking with the "they." In the midst

"They" seldom exist.

of serious conflict, draw together people whom you

trust and ask each of them to list on a separate piece of paper the names of individuals who have talked to them negatively about the issue. Then have one of the most trusted and quiet spoken persons in the group take the names and collate them. You will be surprised to see how few people there are on the combined lists.

Throughout any conflict, keep a steady course and do not let go of the rudder. If you are asked your opinion, give it. Pray and wait for God to work in everyone's heart. Hold a prayer session in which the various parties are encouraged to seek God's leadership. Focus on the vision and mis-

> *Keep you hand firmly on the rudder and do not leave the helm during the storm.*

sion of the church. Keep the conflict in perspective with the overall mission of the church. Continue to bring the people back to the central issue of the church's mission.

Realize that in any conflict relationships usually win out over reason, competence, or rational thought. This preference for relationship over competency is especially true in small congregations with many blood ties. In almost every declining case I have seen, the Controllers are in the seat of making decisions. Even though the majority of the people feel differently, they allow the Controllers to continue because of prior relationships that take precedence over effectiveness. Look for points of agreement and be open to short-term compromise that does not affect the long-term outcome. **mOO**

Don't be surprised if the conflict isn't limited to your congregation. Denominational leaders are notorious for ostracizing those who question and go against the status quo. **mOO** Pastors of all denominations have told me that some of their strongest conflict

163

comes from their denominational leaders. The best thing denominational leaders can do is praise those pastors and churches on the fringe who are doing everything out of step but are effectively leading their people into the twenty-first century.

Keep the flow of information open at all times. Organizations that rely more on values than rules have to open up the flow of information from the top down and the bottom up. They have to give more authority to everyone at every level of the church. Keep the congregation informed on the progress of the pilot ministry. Whenever anyone has a legitimate concern, act on it. Encourage information to flow in and out of the leadership team. Be open to other viewpoints.

Develop a learning loop. As the pilot ministry develops, evaluation is essential. Keep good records of what you are learning and who contributed what. Keep a file folder or computer file for all of the valuable lessons so they can be passed on from person to person.

Permission-giving churches reward those who make mistakes.　　**mOO**　　Permission-giving churches develop synergetic attitudes and policies toward innovation. The clearer the church is about its mission and the more it uses technical support to connect all of the parts of the Body (synergy), the more it will learn and the fewer mistakes it will make. At first, mistakes are part of the learning curve. Accept them, but work to minimize them.

Step Nine—Institutionalization

Once the pilot is successful, a vote to continue may not be necessary because the mem-

> **Protect your core ministries.**

bers have become accustomed to the new ministry. In some cases a few of the Controllers may even be involved in it.

If the pilot project is to be a new core ministry, it is essential to institutionalize it by ensuring that it becomes a new homeostasis.[19] Staff involvement is essential to institutionalize a new core ministry. The new ministry must be able to survive the coming and going of interested lay leaders. Often a church will begin a new ministry based on the interests of a lay person. Over time the ministry becomes a core ministry that is a major entry point into the life of the church. However, when the lay person leaves the church or retires, what is now a core ministry is in jeopardy. Without staff involvement at this point, it usually ceases to exist.

It is better to enhance the part of the core that is working than to protect the core by adding peripherals. George Barna says that most transformation begins by reducing the number of ministries and concentrating on doing a few things well.[20]

Slowly begin to dismantle any organizational structure possible. Practice triage.[21]   moo   As you are able, allow ineffective events or committees to drop. Go out of your way to discontinue anything that is not serving a valid purpose. Try to achieve the lowest possible number of committees. List all of the committees in the church. Next, scratch off those that are needed periodically but not every year. Scratch off those whose elimination would not cause any ministry to cease functioning. Be absolutely brutal in your assessment. Those remaining are the Standing Committees.

Throughout the process the most important question to keep in mind is, How do we accelerate innovation and maintain continuity?[22] Keep tightening and releasing the pressure to become a permission-giving

165

network. Remember, if you move too fast, you drive the members into too much fear. If you move them too slowly, you allow them to be at ease in Zion. Neither is fertile soil for permission-giving churches.

The Quantum Leap

The popular television series *Quantum Leap,* now in syndication is about Sam Beckett, who leaps from one person's body to another in an attempt to help determine the direction of the person's life. Every time a "leap" occurs, Sam is disoriented and needs time to acclimate himself to the new environment.

Developing permission-giving churches is much the same experience. We take a leap into uncharted territory. It is risky business. Like the atomic particle leaping from one orbit to another, developing permission-giving churches is not a guaranteed endeavor. We may fail or we may succeed. There is no guarantee.   moo

However, one thing is certain. What most of our churches are doing at the moment is not developing disciples of Jesus Christ who are willing to live on behalf of people they have not yet met. Like the physicist who peers into the atomic world for the first time and discovers that the old questions no longer work, we know that we need to formulate new questions and look for new solutions if we are going to be effective in the quantum world.

Are you ready to take the quantum leap and begin the long and uncertain road toward the permission-giving church of the future? Go ahead, take the leap. God will catch you, but you might lose your church.

moo

APPENDIXES

Appendix 1

Spiritual Gifts

It may be helpful simply to list the various spiritual gifts mentioned in the Scriptures. We must remember, however, that there is some question as to whether some of these gifts pertained only to the first century, as well as whether or not the only spiritual gifts that exist are those mentioned in the Scriptures. The ones with asterisks I have found to be most helpful in established congregations.

1 Corinthians 12–14

*Wisdom: Equips a person to have insight into how certain knowledge should be applied to specific needs.

*Knowledge: Equips a person to discover, analyze, clarify, and articulate information and concepts essential to the work of the Body of Christ.

*Faith: Equips a person to have so much confidence in God that they never see an impasse—only detours which they can go around in pursuit of accomplishing God's work.

*Prophecy: Equips an individual to proclaim truth in a way people can understand for the purpose of correction, repentance, or nurture. This is not so much fore telling the future as it is being able to draw implications from the Bible to life's situations.

*Teaching: Equips a person to understand and communicate information so that others within the Body learn and grow.

*Helps/Service: Equips a person to accomplish practical and necessary tasks which support and build up the Body. These people usually work alone and behind the scene. Often, this gift has nothing to do with people.

*Administration: Equips a person to bring order to all or part of an organization and to formulate and enact procedures that enhance the function of the organization and support the mission and vision of the Body.

*Discernment: Equips a person to be able to see through phony individuals and ideas. (People with this gift must take care not to be overly judgmental.)

Miracles: Equips a person to accomplish exceptional interventions of God's power to glorify God and give evidence of God's grace.

Healing: Equips a person to be God's channel to restore people to health.

Tongues: Equips a person to speak with unintelligible utterances.

Interpretation: Equips a person to make known to the Body of Christ the message of the person speaking in tongues.

Romans 12

*Leadership (governments): Equips a person to articulate, cast, and share a vision in such a way that the individual members of the Body discover ways in which they can make the vision a reality.

*Exhortation (encouragement): Equips a person to reassure, strengthen, affirm, and offer comfort to those who may be faltering in their faith or who are going through hard times. This is seldom seen as a gift by the person using it.

*Mercy: Equips a person to respond lovingly and compassionately to both the churched and unchurched who are suffering.

*Giving: Equips a person to contribute cheerfully and liberally of his or her material resources so the work of God may spread. (This may be the only gift this person has, and it may not be realized as a gift.)

Ephesians 4

*Evangelism: Equips the person to effectively communicate the story of Jesus Christ so that the unchurched will respond and move toward discipleship. (This person enjoys sharing his or her faith.)

*Shepherding: Equips a person to guide, care for, and nurture individuals or groups in the Body so they can grow in their faith. This person may or may not be an ordained minister; however, this gift assumes a longtime, personal commitment to the spiritual welfare of others.

Apostleship: Equips a person to start new churches and oversee their development.

1 Peter 4

*Hospitality: Equips a person to enjoy opening his or her home to guests and to provide food, fellowship, or shelter.

Other texts on spiritual gifts

*Intercession: Equips a person to pray for an extended period of time on a regular basis for individuals, both the churched and the unchurched, and for specific ministries of the Body (James 5:14-16; 1 Timothy 2:1-2).

*Counseling: Equips a person to effectively listen to people and assist them in their psychological and relational journeys toward wholeness (Matthew 5).

Celibacy: Equips a person to remain single and enjoy it for the sake of the Kingdom (Matthew 19:10-12; 1 Corinthians 7:8).

Exorcism: Equips a person to cast out demons and evil spirits (Matthew 10:1; Luke 10:17-19).

Martyrdom: Equips a person to undergo suffering even to the point of death and to do so while displaying a joyous and victorious attitude that brings glory to God (1 Corinthians 13:1-3).

Appendix 2

ADMINISTRATIVE COUNCIL

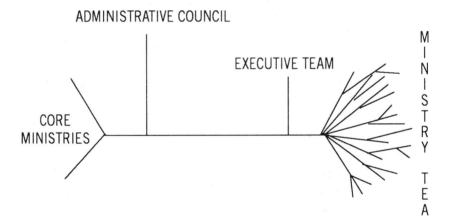

Appendix 3

Permission-giving Readiness Test

Answer the following questions 1–10 with 1 being a total Yes and 10 being a total No.

1. Our church leaders believe that people doing the

actual ministry should make the majority of the decisions that affect how they do their ministry.

2. People at the lowest level of organization in our church should be able to suggest and implement improvements to their own ministry without going through several committees and levels of approval.

3. Each person in the congregation should be free to live out their spiritual gifts in the congregation without getting approval even if it means starting a new ministry.

4. The nature of ministry lends itself to a team-based approach rather than to individual effort.

5. Our leadership is flexible enough to permit restructuring or reorganization so that the organization facilitates the new mission of the church.

6. It is possible to organize ministry so that teams can take responsibility for entire ministries.

7. There is enough complexity in our ministry to allow for initiative and decision making.

8. Our leadership is comfortable with individuals or teams making autonomous, on-the-spot decisions.

9. The laity is interested or willing to organize into teams or small groups.

10. Our key leadership is willing to share its power with those who are not in leadership.

11. Our church has a history of following through on new ideas.

12. Our key lay leadership is willing to radically change its own roles and behavior.

13. Our church is secure enough to guarantee a period of relative stability during which permission-giving can develop.

14. We have adequate resources to support and train our people.

15. Our staff and key lay leadership understand that

becoming a permission-giving church is a lengthy time-consuming, and labor-intensive process that may take five years and is willing to make the investment in time.

16. Our church has a network that could provide information to any lay person anytime.

17. Our lay people have the skills needed to take greater responsibility for the ministries of the church.

18. Our senior pastor is willing to invest in training the team leaders.

19. Our Finance and Trustee Committees should exist to serve the needs of the those trying to implement ministry.

20. Our leaders are more concerned with discovering ways to reach the unchurched than with how those ministries are discovered or implemented.

The lower the score the more able the church is to transform into a permission-giving church.

Under 60   You are ready to shift to a permission-giving church.

61–79   You have some weaknesses in the system. Work on the weaknesses and begin the shift gradually.

Over 80   No need to try to transform the church. Begin exploring your mission, vision, and value statements

NOTES

1. The Sacred Cow

1 Unfortunately Loren Mead did not make this distinction in his book *Transformation Congregations for the Future*. His statement on page 95, "The decision-making processes of religious institutions are mostly controlled by clergy," does not fit into my experience in over five-hundred churches. However, all of his examples are at a higher level of church life than the local church. It is true that clergy clearly control denominational machinery. It is not true that they control the decision-making processes in most established churches. Perhaps Mead is drawing all of his conclusions from his Episcopal or Pentecostal background.

The other thing to note about Mead's argument is that the transformation of a congregation has little if anything to do with the decisions made by the denomination.

2 In the first few drafts I used the word empowerment. I am indebted to Peter Drucker for the encouragement (from reviewing my notes from a personal interview with Drucker at a Leadership Network Conference in 1992) to use words like *responsibility* and *contribution*.

3 For more see Tom Peters, *The Tom Peters Seminar* (New York: Vintage, 1994), chapter 3, page 76. Like many others, he is urging organizations to go beyond mere empowerment to making each person in the organization what he calls a "90 percent entrepreneur."

4 You can reach Bill Easum at 21st Century Strategies, Inc., P.O. Box 549, Port Aransas, Texas 78373.

2. The Quantum Age

1 Limerick and Cunningham wrote in *Managing The New Organization* (San Francisco: Jossey-Bass, 1993), 47, "The idiom that

says 'the only constant thing in the world today is change' turned out to be the ultimate illusion. Even Change changed."

2 Zbigniew Brzezinski, *Out of Control* (New York: Macmillan, 1993), x.

3 Peter Drucker, *The Age of Discontinuity* (New York: Harper Collins, 1969).

4 Alvin Toffler, *The Third Wave* (London: Pan Books, 1981).

5 Harrison Owen, *Spirit: Transformation and Development in Organizations* (Potomac: Abbott Publishing, 1987), 3.

6 For information on Quantum physics for nonscientists read Fred Alan Wolf, *Taking the Quantum Leap* (New York: Harper & Row, 1989). For a more in-depth reading see Frank Tipler, *The Physics of Immortality* (New York: Doubleday, 1994).

7 This is the world of Alfred North Whitehead, Paul Tillich, and Pierre Teilhard De Chardin.

8 In his book *In Search of Schroedinger's Cat: Quantum Physics and Reality* (New York: Bantam Books, 1984), 227ff, John Gribbin describes an experiment of Alain Aspect in which two electrons were paired together and tested to see if, once correlated, they could maintain their connection over a distance. Electrons are correlated by pairing their spins so that the sum of the spins is zero. They spin along an axis of rotation that is either up or down. Remember, in Quantum physics the axes exist only as potentials until we measure them. A fixed spin cannot be given an electron until it is measured. In the two electrons that are paired together, if one spins up the other will spin down, or if right the other will spin left. During the experiment, the electrons are separated. Still, the moment an electron is measured for its spin, the other changes direction. Measure the spin of one, and even though separated, the other changes to the opposite direction. The quantum question is, "How does the second electron, so far away, know which axis we choose to measure?"

9 Margaret J. Wheatley, *Leadership and the New Science* (San Francisco: Berrett-Koehler, 1993), 68.

10 People representing three theological traditions have recognized the significance of the relational universe. The first is

Teilhard de Chardin, a geologist turned Christian thinker. He provided an alternative within Roman Catholicism, and whose theological system has been seminal to global, environmental theologians. The second is Alfred North Whitehead, whose philosophical writings motivated a whole range of "process thought." In North America, the philosophical side of Whitehead's work has been led by Charles Hartshorne, while the theological side of this work has been lead by John B. Cobb, Jr. The third is Paul Tillich, whose metaphysics and philosophy of science has been largely ignored in North America until the last two decades. Whitehead's and Tillich's thoughts on "participation" are the first serious theological attempts at describing the faith in the quantum world.

These theologians represent a distinct departure from the world view of Aristotle and the theology of Thomas Aquinas toward the mystical world view of Plato and the theology of Augustine. Their theological debt is to people like Bonaventure, Erasmus, and Thomas Moore. They were greatly influenced by the sixteenth century mystic Jacob Boehme, the German idealist Friedreich Schelling, the nineteenth century French "Life Philosophy" movement by Henri Bergson, and the scientific explorations of British neo-Platonists such as Einstein. Theologically, Wesley and the Wesleyan movement is the heir to Erasmus, and perhaps the most open of all religious movements to recognize the significance of larger world views in the formation of faith.

It could well be that in the twenty-first century the decisive influences on personal spirituality could come as much from the emerging understanding of a relational universe in which the infinite and the finite intersect in unexpected ways, as from the historic creeds and biblical interpretations.

[11] This is the Gaia hypothesis, which is on the fringe of accepted practice but is gaining credibility. See Howard Snyder, *EarthCurrents* (Nashville: Abingdon Press, 1995).

[12] Fritjof Capra, *The Turning Point: Science, Society, and the Rising Culture* (New York: Bantam Books, 1983).

[13] The work of Ilya Prigogine answered the question, "If entropy is the rule, why does life flourish?" He coined the phrase "dissipative structures." Dissipation describes the process by which energy gradually fades away. However, he often observed, it did not lead to the demise of the system, but to the creation of a new system better suited to the present environment.

[14] Frank Tippler, *The Physics of Immortality* (New York: Doubleday, 1994). Tippler argues that theology is a branch of physics and that physicists can infer by calculation (reductionism) the existence of God and the resurrection of the dead. Humans are a very complicated computer program. The soul is also a computer program run by the brain.

3. The Controllers

[1] The first century church was not without its Controllers. See Acts 10–11 and Acts 14–16.

[2] In my last book *Dancing With Dinosaurs,* I wrote: "Bureaucracies and traditional practices are the major causes of decline in most denominations in North America." William M. Easum, *Dancing With Dinosaurs* (Nashville: Abingdon Press, 1993), 14.

[3] For a lengthy discussion on the role of Trustees as servants see chapter 3 in Robert Greenleaf, *Servant Leadership* (New York: Paulist Press, 1977).

4. The Connection and Foundation

[1] For many older church leaders, the body is often associated with sinful pleasures. It will help if you finally lay these ideas aside.

[2] The Scriptures do mention the "household of God," but always in relationship to all of God's people, never in any of the infinite varieties family is used today. The "household of God" includes singles too, since it is not used in the familial sense. Almost one-half of North America is now single. See Ephesians 3–5.

[3] Janet Fishburn, *Confronting the Idolatry of the Family* (Nashville: Abingdon Press, 1991), 86. Although Fishburn does not understand the concerns of the Baby Buster or the Church Growth movement, she gives a compelling argument for abandoning the Victorian emphasis on the "family pew." Readers will also benefit from her comments about the declining role of Sunday school and the need for pastors to be spiritual leaders.

[4] Howard Snyder, *Models of the Kingdom* (Nashville: Abingdon Press, 1991).

[5] I am indebted at this point to a book given to me by a good friend and member of the congregation where I served Christ between 1969–93. Philip Yancey and Dr. David Brand, *Fearfully and Wonderfully Made* (Grand Rapids: Zondervan, 1980).

[6] Red blood cells, muscle cells, cartilage cells, bone cells, fat cells, brain cells, nerve cells, sex cells, and so on. Each of these appear very different under the microscope.

[7] DNA is so compact that all the genes in a person's body could fit into an ice cube, but if the DNA were unwound and joined end to end it would stretch from the earth to the sun and back more than four hundred times.

[8] The Scriptures describe a wide variety of spiritual gifts. The primary passages are 1 Corinthians 12–14; 1 Peter 4; Ephesians 4; and Romans 12.

5. Permission-Giving Churches

[1] G. K. Chesterton, *Orthodoxy* (Garden City, N.Y.: Doubleday, 1959), 95.

[2] At Colonial Hills, everyone had permission to begin a new ministry as long as it didn't violate our corporate values. All a person had to do was present his or her case to a lay leader or staff person and be willing to take responsibility for the new ministry. When the staff member or lay leader on rare occasion refused permission, the person could go to the Executive Team and present his or her case. It could make decisions based on the strategic plan that existed. If

the request did not violate our corporate culture or any of its strategic goals, permission was granted.

[3] I doubt if any permission-giving church would attempt to build, or relocate, or develop a budget without taking a vote. Common sense, or should I say, uncommon sense, exists in these churches.

6. Discovering Our Place in God's World

[1] Stanley J. Menking and Barbara Wendland, *God's Partners: Lay Christians at Work* (Valley Forge: Judson, 1993), 20. This is a delightful book that will give help to many lay persons. Two people, one a lay person and one a seminary professor, dialogue with each other.

[2] Almost all of the material on spiritual gifts is from Paul.

[3] Wayne A. Meeks, *The First Urban Christians* (New Haven: Yale University Press, 1983).

[4] Martha Ellen Stortz, *Pastor Power* (Nashville: Abingdon Press, 1993).

[5] Wayne A. Meeks, *The First Urban Christians* (New Haven: Yale University Press, 1983).

[6] Loren Mead, *The Once and Future Church* (Washington, D.C.: Alban Institute, 1991).

[7] William M. Easum, *Discovering Our Place in God's World* (Port Aransas, Tex.: 21st Century Strategies, 1989).

[8] Bruce Bugbee, *Network* (Pasadena, Calif.: Fuller Institute, 1994).

[9] C. Peter Wagner, *Spiritual Gifts Discovery* (Pasadena, Calif.: Fuller Institute, 1978).

[10] William M. Easum, *Discovering Our Place in God's World* (Port Aransas, Tex.: 21st Century Strategies, 1989).

7. Permission-Giving Leaders

[1] For more on this subject see William M. Easum, *Dancing With Dinosaurs* (Nashville: Abingdon Press, 1993) and Loren Mead, *The Once and Future Church* (Washington, D.C.: Alban Institute, 1991).

[2] For more see Charles Hampden-Turner, *Creating Corporate Culture* (Reading, Mass.: Addison-Wesley, 1990).

[3] Murry Bowen, *Family Therapy in Clinical Practice* (Northvale, N.J.: Jason Aronson, 1985). Edwin Friedman, a rabbi and family system therapist, as well as student of Murry Bowen, has popularized the concept through his book *Generation to Generation* (New York: Guilford Press, 1985).

[4] In his Pulitzer Prize-winning book, Burns distinguished between "transformational" and "transactional" leaders. Transformational leaders created new situations and systems; transactional leaders work in incremental, evolutionary changes. J. M. Burns, *Leadership* (New York: Harper Collins, 1978). Burns's distinction is much like that of Zaleznk who argues that leaders create images that excite others to develop new options; whereas managers maintain systems by enabling others and limiting options. Managers relate to roles, leaders relate intuitively and empathetically to others. A. A. Zaleznik, "Managers and Leaders: Are They Different?" Harvard Business Review 55, no. 3 (1977): 67-78.

[5] I have chosen to use Mentor/Birther. Some people do not like the word mentor because it implies someone has authority over another. This is true. Think of the best teachers you know. You learned from them because you gave them authority. Mentors have authority only because others give them the authority. Mentors never impose authority on others. It is either given, or the mentoring relationship never begins. Others do not like the word mentor because it tends to perpetuate male leadership. One could also refer to Midwife.

[6] My calculation is that 51 percent of Jesus' time was spent with the Twelve.

[7] I almost chose not to use the word "call" because it carries so much baggage. It almost always refers only to clergy. The way I am using it refers to every Christian.

[8] W. G. Bennis and B. Nanus, *Leaders: The Strategies for Taking Charge* (New York: HarperCollins, 1985).

[9] Peter Drucker, *Post-Capitalist Society* (New York: Harper Business, 1993), 53.

[10] For more on why planning is not as important in the quantum world see Henry Mintzberg, *The Rise and Fall of Strategic Planning* (New York: The Free Press, 1994). For information on perhaps the best form of strategic planning see Peter Schwartz, *The Art of The Long View* (New York: Currency-Doubleday, 1991).

[11] Co-dependent leaders (1) find fulfillment not in what they do but in how people respond to them; (2) need people to need them; (3) wait on the will of the people to form consensus, prefer peace over progress; (4)are insecure about their own ministry and need others to set their agenda; (5) allow the congregation to go wherever it wants to go or be anything that it wants to be; (6) do not have a personal vision for the congregation; (7) never make an entrepreneurial decision; (8) always want to hear one more opinion before taking action; (9) are afraid to delegate major tasks to others; (10) tend to be more afraid than courageous.

[12] Peter Senge, *The Fifth Discipline* (New York: Doubleday, 1990).

[13] Peter Koestenbaum, *Leadership: The Inner Side of Greatness* (San Francisco: Jossey-Bass, 1991).

[14] Told to me in a phone conversation December, 1994. The game he mentioned is "Myst." I subsequently purchased the game and discovered what he meant. Sweet is not the first person I've heard recommending video games as a way into the quantum world.

[15] You can find several excercises in Joel Barker, *Paradigms;* Peter Koestenbaum, *Leadership: The Inner Side of Greatness;* and Stanley Davis, *Future Perfect.*

[16] Tom Peters, *Thriving on Chaos* (New York: Harper Collins, 1988).

[17] Richard Wellins, *Empowered Teams* (San Francisco: Jossey-Bass, 1991).

[18] William M. Easum, *The Church Growth Handbook* (Nashville: Abingdon Press, 1990).

8. Permission-Giving Networks

[1] Gifford and Elizabeth Pinchot in their book *The End of Bureaucracy and the Rise of the Intelligent Organization* suggest

that bureaucracy is in ill-repute today for two reasons. First, the nature of work has changed. We have moved from unskilled work to knowledge work, from repetitive tasks to innovation and caring, from individual work to teamwork, from functional work to project work, from single-skill to multi-skilled, from the power of bosses to the power of people's needs, from coordination from above to coordination among peers. Second, there has been a revolutionary change in the structure of our relationships. Information-intensive jobs require in-depth relationships and cross-skill training. Bureaucracy is incapable of adapting to either of these fundamental changes in our society.

2 For more information see William M. Easum, *How to Reach Baby Boomers* (Nashville: Abingdon Press, 1992), 17-23; and William M. Easum, *Dancing With Dinosaurs* (Nashville: Abingdon Press, 1993), 23-34.

3 Stanley Davis, *Future Perfect* (New York: Addison-Wesley, 1982), 5.

4 According to some, the strength of bulletin boards is also their weakness. The ability for anyone, anytime, anyplace to access and input information into the system means that the time will come when the system may collapse under the weight of its own information. Someone will have to clean out the garbage or there will be so much that no one can find anything.

5 Harrison Owen, *Open Space Technology* (Potomac: Abbott Publishing, 1992).

6 Marilyn Ferguson, *The Aquarian Conspiracy: Personal and Social Transformation in the 1980s* (Los Angeles: Tarcher, 1980), 213.

7 Effective denominational structures will have one thing in common—they will be designed to facilitate ministry in the local churches and not to take care of them or do things that the local churches do not have courage or sense enough to do themselves.

8 Kirbyjon Caldwell said this at the 1994 Leadership Network in Minneapolis, Minnesota. Kirbyjon Caldwell is pastor of Windsor United Methodist Church, one of the largest and fastest growing churches in the denomination.

9 For more information see *Fortune*, "The End of the Job" (September 19, 1994), 62–74.

10 Peter Senge, *The Fifth Discipline* (New York: Doubleday, 1990).

11 I call these people "fringe people." See William M. Easum, *Dancing With Dinosaurs* (Nashville: Abingdon Press, 1993). See also M. Mitchell Waldrop, *Complexity: The Emerging Science at the Edge of Order and Chaos* (New York: Simon & Schuster, 1992), 12. Waldrop is a member of the Santa Fe Institute, an iconoclastic think tank, that has a deep impatience with the kind of linear reductionist thinking of Newtonian physics. In his book he describes how chaos emerges into order.

12 Three of the best books on this subject are: James Gleich, *Chaos: Making a New Science* (New York: Viking, 1987); Margaret J. Wheatley, *Leadership and the New Science* (San Francisco: Berrett-Koehler, 1992); and Tom Peters, *Thriving on Chaos* (New York: HarperCollins, 1988).

13 See Margaret J. Wheatley, *Leadership and the New Science* (San Francisco: Berrett-Koehler, 1992), 79. Wheatley shows a picture of the Three-Winged Bird: A Chaotic Strange Attractor. Through the use of a computer, the image of a simple nonlinear equation that went through millions of iterations was plotted as in three dimensional computer phase space. Over time the shape of a beautiful bird emerged.

14 Harrison Owen, *Riding the Tiger* (Potomac: Abbott 1991), 29.

15 The importance of developing relationships and information is the primary reason why most growing churches are experiencing longer pastorates. The longer the pastor stays, the deeper the relationships, and thus the greater the sum of knowledge in the church.

16 Alvin Toffler speaks about "Skunkwork Organizations" in *Powershift* (New York: Bantam Books, 1990), 196-97.

17 Drucker sees this event as the end of "four hundred years of history in which the sovereign nation-state was the main, and often the only, actor on the political stage." See Peter Drucker, *Post-Capitalist Society* (New York: Harper Business, 1993), 9. The same can be said for established denomina-

tions. They will continue for some time to come, but they will probably never regain their dominance in the North American religious landscape.

[18] Leadership Network, Box 9100, Tyler, Texas 75711, 800-765-5323; Willow Creek Association, Box 3188, South Barrington, Illinois 60011-3188, 708-765-0070; Teaching Church Network, P. O. Box 39282, Minneapolis, MN 55439-0208, 612-942-9866, fax 612-949-6711.

9. Self-Organizing Ministry Teams

[1] These figures are based on over four-hundred local church consultations where pastors were surveyed regarding these questions.

[2] I first wrote about Ministry Teams in *How to Reach Baby Boomers* (Nashville: Abingdon Press, 1992).

[3] The widespread use of teams in North America began in the 1980s when industries like auto and steel began forming quality circles, in which workers met weekly or monthly to discuss ways to improve quality (do not make the mistake of comparing quality circles with a congregation's favorite way of wasting time—brainstorming). See David Limerick and Bert Cunningham, *Managing the New Organization* (San Francisco: Jossey-Bass, 1993) for an opposite viewpoint.

[4] One of the opening comments in his 1982 written report to Colonial Hills.

[5] Jessica Moffatt talked with me in January, 1995 at a Large Church Initiative sponsored by the United Methodist Church in Tulsa, Oklahoma.

[6] For more information on cell churches see the magazine "Cell Church," 14925 Memorial Drive, Suite 101, Houston, Texas 77079.

[7] The term was coined by Gifford and Elizabeth Pinchot in their book *Intrapreneuring* (San Francisco: Berrett-Koehler, 1993).

[8] "The Trouble with Teams," *Fortune* (September 5, 1994), 86–92. Many feel that, in time, self-organizing networks may replace most forms of hierarchy and bureaucracy.

Organization will focus on (1) the whole, as opposed to the parts, and (2) the relationships (interconnectedness and compatibility) between the parts, as opposed to isolated compartments or linear operations and thought. Span of control, levels of rank and expertise, and competition will be replaced with permission-giving, egalitarian relationships, and cooperation. None will be more important to permission-giving churches than the Ministry Teams.

[9] According to the 1994 Fall edition of the Alban Institute newsletter, their most popular seminar is "Consulting with Severely Conflicted Churches." This is sad, because I believe that the more a church focuses on conflict management, the faster that church will die.

[10] Those wishing to know more about small group ministry see William M. Easum, *Dancing With Dinosaurs* (Nashville: Abingdon Press, 1993).

[11] These teams are not what some call self-directed teams. See Richard Wellins, William Byham, and Jeanne Wilson, *Empowered Teams* (San Francisco: Jossey-Bass, 1991). Ministry Teams are permanent units. Most others come and go as needed.

[12] For more information subscribe to *Christian Computing*, P.O. Box 198, Reamer, MO 64083.

[13] For a brief time in the 1970s human resource accounting flourished and then vanished, probably because managers still conceived profits based on the ratio of body count to the number of sales. Churches and denominational leaders often make the same mistake.

[14] Even though some question the value of psychographic material, I have found it helpful, especially when the information is linked with Focus Groups.

[15] Several firms provide excellent demographic data. Percept (formerly CIDS), 151 Kalmus Drive, Suite A-104, Costa Mesa, AZ. I use this firm because it is designed primarily for church use. Stanley J. Menking, presently with the Perkins School of Theology, is the best I have seen at analyzing the data. He has combined the Percept demographics with the Tex Sample analysis of left, middle, and right cul-

ture, in *U.S. Lifestyles and Mainline Churches* (Louisville, Ky.: Westminster/John Knox, 1990). Perkins School of Theology at SMU, Continuing Education Department, P.O. Box 133, Dallas, Texas 75275-0133, 214-768-2251. Donnelley Marketing Information Services, 70 Seaview Ave., P.O. Box 10250, Stamford, CT 06904, 800-866-2255. Claritas, 201 North Union Street, Alexandria, VA 22314, 703-683-8300.

The monthly magazine *American Demographics* is the best on the market. 800-828-1133.

[16] I have often heard my good friend from Canada, Tom Bandy, ask this question. Tom is on the Division of Congregational Mission and Evangelism of the United Church of Canada. Tom is one of the most astute people at the denominational level I have encountered in any established denomination in North America.

10. The Steering Team

[1] The early church had the practice of "casting lots" (rolling dice) to determine some forms of leadership in the church (see Acts). At least, this practice assured that money, desire for power, or popularity did not play a part in the selection of leadership. Some times I think we would be far better off today if we too simply rolled the dice.

[2] In *How to Reach Baby Boomers* (Nashville: Abingdon Press, 1992), I called this group the Executive Team. I would not use this term today because it sounds as if ministry is directed in a top-down manner.

[3] Charles Hampden-Turner, *Creating Corporate Culture* (Reading, Mass.: Addison-Wesley, 1990), 12.

[4] Steven Covey makes a distinction between Values and Principles. However, for our purpose, I see no difference. Actually, Covey took his principles from classic Christian Virtues.

[5] For more see William M. Easum, *The Church Growth Handbook* (Nashville: Abingdon Press, 1990).

6 Peter Drucker, *Post-Capitalist Society* (New York: Harper Business, 1993), 53.

7 For more on the difference between Vision and Mission Statements see George Barna, *Church Marketing* (Ventura: Regal Books, 1992), 135-6.

8 I have intentionally not made a reference to any form of Strategic planning because too often it is just another way church leaders control what happens from the top down. As Mintzberg said in *The Rise and Fall of Strategic Planning*, "Perhaps the clearest theme in the planning literature is its obsession with control—of decisions and strategies of the present and the future, or thoughts and actions, or workers and managers, or markets and customers." Henry Mintzberg, *The Rise and Fall of Strategic Planning* (New York: Free Press, 1994), 201-2. Minztberg gives an excellent, but tedious, critical review of most of the basic forms of strategic planning.

11. Transformation

1 This is according to my annual survey of churches that I have worked with over the years.

2 Tom Bandy and I developed these together during a three-week tour of Canada in 1993.

3 David Keirsey and Marilyn Bates, *Please Understand Me* (Del Mar, Calif.: Promethean, 1978).

4 For information call Birkman International, Inc., 713-623-2760.

5 In many ways steps 2 through 4 can be compared to "force field analysis."

6 Homeostasis is that part of systems thinking that says left to itself all systems will return to their former state. Systems have a life force that will do whatever is necessary to keep anything from changing.

7 If you show me proof that you have purchased a copy of *The Church Growth Handbook,* I will send you an updated copy of the Ministry Audit for a charge of $10.00.

8 Charles Handy, *The Age of Paradox* (Harvard Business School Press, 1994).

9   The community was Spring Hill, Florida.

10 Several firms provide excellent demographic data. Percept (formerly CIDS), 151 Kalmus Drive, Suite A-104, Costa Mesa, AZ 92626, 714-957-1282. I use this firm because it is designed primarily for church use. Stanley J. Menking, presenty with Perkins School of Theology, is the best I have seen at anayzing the data. He has combined the Percept demographics with the Tex Sample's analysis of left, middle, and right culture, in *U.S. Lifestyles and Mainline Churches*. Perkins School of Theology at SMU, Continuing Education Department, P. O. Box 133, Dallas, Texas. 75275-0133, 214-768-2251.

Donnelley Marketing Information Services, 70 Seaview Ave., P. O. Box 10250, Stamford, CT 06904, 800-866-2255.

Claritas, 201 North Union Union Street Alexandria, VA 22314, 703-683-8300.

The monthly magazine *American Demographics* is the best on the market, 800-828-1133.

11 Rural churches need a demographic study that covers at least one hour driving time in all directions around their church, unless some natural boundary prohibits this (e.g., river, mountains, or other boundary). Most other churches need a study of the area that can be covered in a thirty minute drive time during rush-hour traffic.

12 For more information on Focus Groups see Jane Templeton, *A Guide for Marketing and Advertising Professionals* (American Demographics, P.O. Box 68, Ithaca, NY 14851, 800-828-1133); and George Barna, *Church Marketing* (Ventura, Calif.: Regal Books, 1992).

13 For more information see Jane Templeton, *Focus Groups: A Guide for Marketing and Advertising Professionals* (Ithaca, N.Y.: American Demographics). George Barna, *Church Marketing* (Ventura, Calif.: Regal Books, 1992).

14 For an excellent view of the pastor as spiritual leader see Janet Fishburn, *Confronting the Idolatry of the Family* (Nashville: Abingdon Press, 1991), chapters 8–9 and the epilogue.

[15] Guy Benveniste, *The Twenty-First Century Organization* (San Francisco: Jossey-Bass, 1994), 91ff.

[16] Judith Bardkwick, *Danger in the Comfort Zone* (New York: American Management Association, 1991).

[17] The best writing on shared vision I have seen is Peter Senge, *Fifth Discipline* (New York: Doubleday, 1990), chapter 11.

[18] For more information order *L.I.F.E. Groups* from 21st Century Strategies, Inc., P.O. Box 549, Port Aransas, Texas 78373.

[19] This stage is similar to Kurt Lewin's "refreezing" stage. Refreezing involves training people to function in the new paradigm and to improve the quality of the new homeostasis. Kurt Lewin, *Dynamic Theory of Personality* (New York: McGraw Hill, 1935) and *Resolving Social Conflicts* (New York: Harper and Bros., 1948).

[20] George Barna, *Turnaround Churches* (Ventura, Calif.: Regal Books, 1993).

[21] I first talked about triage in *How to Reach Baby Boomers* (Nashville: Abingdon Press, 1992).

[22] Benveniste, *The Twenty-First Century Organization*, 55.